# THE
# BALANCED
# ENTREPRENEUR

## Finding and perfecting ideas to generate financing, freedom, fun, and fortune!

## MARK SIMON Ph.D.

**Entrepreneur & University Professor of Entrepreneurship**

## PRACTICAL STARTUP STRATEGIES BASED ON SCHOLARLY RESEARCH, WRITTEN FOR REAL PEOPLE

Published by: Entrepreneurial Life Publications
4877 Menominee Ln, Clarkston, MI 48348

Document Title: The Balanced Entrepreneur
Subtitle: Finding and Perfecting Ideas to Generate Financing, Freedom, Fun, and Fortune
ISBN-13: 978-0983293606
ISBN-10: 0983293600
First edition: September, 2011

Interior Design by Alison Rayner

**Trade marks**

All brand names and product names referred to in this book are trademarks, registered trademarks and service marks of their particular owners. The publisher is not connected with any of the products, services or vendors referred to in this book.

**Disclaimers**

This publication is intended to provide accurate and reliable information regarding the subject matter covered. It is sold with the understanding that the author and publisher are not engaged in giving professional services advice. The advice in this book may not be suitable for your business situation. The author and publisher specifically disclaim any liability that is incurred from the use or application of the contents in this book. You should consult with a professional where appropriate. Neither the author nor the publisher shall be liable for any loss or commercial damages, either implied or explicit.

**Visit our website at:**

# TheBalancedEntrepreneur.com

# TABLE OF CONTENTS

• • •

# FOREWORD

• • •

## Realistic results

Despite decades of starting organizations and researching entrepreneurship, I will not make some of the claims that others do. I cannot teach you how to make five figures a week from week one, while putting nothing down and while working fewer than two days a week!

But read on if you want reasonable, well researched strategies to help you find, perfect and finance your business ideas. While not miraculous, these strategies are likely to significantly increase your profits, enjoyment and free time!

## Startup strategies based on practical experience and scholarly research, but written for real people

Given my Ph.D. in Entrepreneurship from Georgia State University, I often write scholarly research articles in academic language for other professors. But this book is for people like you, who want advice they can implement right away. So I created an enjoyable read that doesn't go on and on about any one study's findings.

Realize, though, that despite the book's conversational tone, all of its suggestions are backed by dozens of rigorous research studies and screened through my real world entrepreneurial experiences.

If you want to learn more about the academic underpinnings of the strategies in the book, you can chat with me at thebalancedentrepreneur. com. But fair warning, I love talking about this stuff, so beware of what you wish for!

Hope you enjoy reading this book as much as I enjoyed writing it!

• • •

# INTRODUCTION

• • •

## Who was this book written for?

After working for your company for years, do you now have to worry about losing your job, or have they cut you already? Would a little security be nice? Even if you feel secure, are you tired of the boss looking over your shoulder? Perhaps you want the freedom to implement your ideas rather than having to beg for approval. And just maybe, after winning the fight for approval and having an idea work, you think it would be nice if you received some tangible and intangible recognition. On top of it all, are you just making ends meet, and can't seem to set aside enough cash for those little extras that make life worth living?

Maybe you're thinking of starting your own business to solve these problems. You've wanted to do so for the longest time, but some of the concerns below are holding you back.

1. You're not sure you have a good enough idea.
2. You're worried about the risks involved.
3. You're afraid of the demands and hours required.
4. You don't know how to get financing.

If anything written above describes your situation, then you need to read this book NOW. The book represents a new and better method of creating your startup. It explains how to conceive of a great new idea or how to systematically tweak your existing idea. It also explains how to maximize your wealth and minimize your risk, while simultaneously making sure you enjoy the process and have enough time for a great life outside of the business. As importantly, it also explains how to get financing.

The strategies I'm about to share with you are very accessible to people without a lot of business experience as well as to those with an extensive business background, such as an MBA. The strategies are useful for everyone who wants to start their own business, but

1. doesn't yet have an idea,
2. only has a vague idea that needs work,
3. has a well defined idea, or
4. is in the process of writing a plan for a startup.

Which of the categories above describes you? Even if you are not quite ready to start your business yet, but think one day you might, the book is still for you. There are easy steps you can take RIGHT NOW that will radically improve your future, by making your business more profitable, enjoyable, and financeable, when you do start it.

## Planning: The outdated approach vs. the new "balanced entrepreneur" method.

Over the decades, an approach to planning has arisen which is outdated and does not serve most of your needs. It came into being because entrepreneurs often require outside capital to start their business. Before providing any funds, however, backers have to be convinced that they should invest. Thus, planning focused on writing a document FOR FUNDERS, showing them that your venture would meet THEIR NEEDS. Planning didn't focus on *your* desires.

But aren't funders' and *your* goals the same? The good news is that like you, they want your venture to make money. The bad news: they are not concerned whether you invest every penny you have and will lose your house if the venture fails. In fact, they like that idea, believing it shows commitment. And while they are not bad people, how do you think they will react if your plan focuses on ways you could cut down your hours at work, so you could have a great marriage???? I think we all know the answer to that one. Funders also are not overly concerned with whether you love or hate going into work each day. Even worse, some funders are satisfied if 70% of the startups they invest in fail, so long as 10% hit it big. Are you happy with a 70% percent chance of failure? While **SOME** aspects of a funder focused method of planning might be helpful, it can leave you with a business an investor likes but you don't. Is it any wonder we refer to the approach as outdated?

It could be okay to use this approach if you supplement it with planning how your business idea can generate the lifestyle you want. But, unfortunately, the outdated approach is so dominant, it is the only approach entrepreneurs use. Not only do entrepreneurs forget to plan for themselves, but even if they did, almost no material exists to help them through the process. Thus the need for the "balanced entrepreneur" method of venture planning.

Before going any further, to avoid any misunderstanding, I need to stress two crucial points. **The balanced entrepreneur method of startup planning will:**

1. **lead you to making more money, and**
2. **make it easier to fund your startup.**

But it accomplishes these two things while making sure you build a startup that gives you more financial security, more freedom, and more fun. How is this "magic" accomplished, you ask? The explanation is so simple it is almost embarrassing. This book only suggests a strategy or piece of advice if it is likely to increase your wealth **and** make it easier to get funding **and** help you to build a business that you can enjoy; one where you can truly be the boss. Any idea which can't accomplish all three goals went into my trash can. Because the outdated approach to planning is so focused on the investor, almost no one has systematically studied which strategies can simultaneously meet their needs and yours – but they are out there and I've gathered them all in this book.

So plainly stated, the new "Balanced Entrepreneur" method of startup planning involves shaping your business idea **at the outset**, so that it meets your needs. Your initial idea, and how you start pursuing it, impacts the business for years to come. Imagine baking a cake. You start by adding salt when the recipe demands sugar, using sour cream when it calls for milk, and putting in lard when butter is required. Starting with the wrong ingredients is almost impossible to overcome. Your cake is destined to be a culinary disaster. Just like cooks must begin with the right ingredients to end up with a scrumptious cake, entrepreneurs must start with ideas that have certain characteristics to build a business that leads to an enjoyable business life and profits.

After decades of study, I've uncovered ten strategies that are key to the balanced entrepreneur method. These strategies need to be incorporated into your startup ideas. Omitting even one can lead to a huge financial struggle, sleepless nights, hundred hour work weeks, a ruined personal life, and missed opportunities. Many entrepreneurs never recover, and those who do, battle for years. Alternatively, starting with an idea that has all the right characteristics from day one, can lead to the ultimate lifestyle including riches, getting the funds you need, loving your work, and free time to pursue your other passions, be they travel, family or a hobby. **SO GET IT RIGHT AT THE START!**

## My Background

I know I am promising a lot, but my unique background allows me to deliver. The strategies I've developed stem from decades of experience founding my own ventures AND studying thousands of articles and books on entrepreneurship AND coaching hundreds of budding entrepreneurs.

My immediate family and I have founded ten startups among us – every one of which has been successful. These ranged from my wilderness canoe trip business to charitable foundations, to importing of gift and decorative accessories from South America, to a venture capital funded high technology startup. These experiences generated powerful insights that only "living a venture" can provide.

But even in-depth experience with ten ventures would not allow me to develop the strategies in this book. To make sure the principles I believed generated my own success are universal truths all entrepreneurs could count on, I learned how to perform research by getting a Ph.D. in entrepreneurship from Georgia State University. For the last twenty years, I have been reviewing thousands of entrepreneurship articles and conducting rigorous studies to uncover and validate startup strategies that lead to both financial success **and** the ultimate lifestyle for a wide range of entrepreneurs.

Finally, I've tested these ideas with the hundreds of clients and entrepreneurship students I teach and coach. This allowed me to make sure that the ideas could be easily implemented and provide others with a great life. It is only the synergistic blend of all three of my roles that allowed me to uncover success strategies that are powerful, can be applied to anyone's idea, and are easy to execute.

So as you read this, do you wonder how I have managed to research entrepreneurship, teach classes, and coach hundreds of budding entrepreneurs, all while starting new ventures? And how I am able to do all this and build a great family life, rich in recreation and travel? More importantly, how can you achieve similar success and flexibility in your life? This book, "The Balanced Entrepreneur: Finding and Perfecting Ideas to Generate Financing, Freedom, Fun, and Fortune" holds the answer.

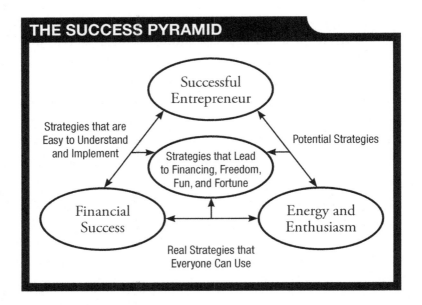

## The Book Contents

Each of this book's chapters emphasizes one of the ten strategies that comprise my new method of startup planning. Each strategy increases profits and generates at least one other benefit, such as:

1. lowering risks,
2. enhancing flexibility,
3. boosting job enjoyment,
4. increasing free time, and
5. making financing easier to obtain.

In truth, however, these benefits are so interrelated that each of the strategies plays at least some role in achieving all or nearly all of the benefits above.

Part One of the book, Finding my Idea, contains two chapters. The first chapter is, **PERSONAL GOALS:** LOVING MY LIFE

AS "THE BOSS." It identifies the first crucial step regarding generating ideas, a step that most people don't take. As a result of this omission, instead of becoming the "boss" of their own work life, these individuals end up working 120 hours a week, putting out constant fires, working on tasks they don't enjoy, and making less than they would if they were working for someone else. In contrast, if you take this step, you are much more likely to truly end up the boss. You will be in control, making lots of money, liking, or dare I say it, loving what you do every day, and having the freedom (and the cash) to have a life outside of the business.

The second chapter is, **THE IDEA:** FINDING IT. If one of the issues holding you back from pursuing your dreams is that you don't have an idea for a venture, this is the chapter you may need most. By the time you are finished with it, your problem will change from not having an idea, to wondering which of the many ideas you are excited about should be explored first.

Part Two of the book, Perfecting my Idea, contains four chapters that help you perfect your idea. Chapter three, **COMPETING I:** ELIMINATING LOW PROFIT, HIGH RISK IDEAS explains why entrepreneurs end up with ventures and lives far different from, and WORSE than, they anticipated. Namely, they completely misunderstand the nature of their competition. This chapter leads to critical insights about rivals that may suggest important ways you need to modify your idea.

Chapter four is, **COMPETING II:** USING THREE TACTICS TO INCREASE MY FREEDOM AND WEALTH. First, the chapter describes the major strategy your venture must pursue to provide you with a better life. Next, it describes three specific tactics you can use to execute that strategy and explains how to avoid traps associated with each way. The chapter will show you how to assess whether your idea incorporates one of the tactics, and if not, how you can correct that.

In chapter five, **THE INDUSTRY:** AVOIDING DANGEROUS TRAPS, I share one strategy regarding industries that so many forget to mention. Understanding and acting on this insight is one hundred percent guaranteed to radically magnify your chance of success and decrease your risk. It will also save you years of struggle.

Chapter six, **MARKETING:** EMPLOYING TECHNIQUES TO INCREASE MY FREE TIME AND DECREASE MY COSTS, explains how, paradoxically, "doing less" will actually generate more money. As importantly, by "doing less" you will minimize your risk, enjoy work more, and have the potential for a great life outside of work. In addition, it explains how to decrease the amount of startup capital you need, and provides the single BEST method for getting it. After reading this chapter you will be able to systematically trim the components of your idea that aren't needed and enhance those that produce benefits.

The third part of the book, Launching my Idea, transports you from focusing on the idea to putting an actual company together. Chapter seven, **THE ORGANIZATION:** SHAPING MY COMPANY TO INCREASE MY FLEXIBILITY AND FUN, gives you a balanced entrepreneur strategy that will absolutely determine whether you will end up miserable or ecstatic. And even though after hearing this strategy it seems obvious, almost no entrepreneurs, scholars, or consultants know it. And fewer than ten of the hundreds of business books and thousands of academic and magazine articles I've read refer to the strategy. I'm not exaggerating. Yet this single strategy can have a greater impact on your future happiness than anything else you've heard – ever.

Chapter eight, **FINANCING I:** DECREASING MY NEED FOR FUNDING, greatly extends the ideas introduced in several of the previous chapters, by showing you how to further decrease your need for up front investments. In addition, it teaches you how to avoid a time consuming, unpleasant, and draining search for cash throughout the life of your business, so you can focus on enjoying your work life and making the business grow.

Chapter nine is, **FINANCING II:** RAISING MONEY MORE EASILY. It provides many novel methods for getting financing that most other entrepreneurship resources overlook. Many of the sources provide cash at less interest or for less ownership than more common well known resources. Perhaps more importantly the chapter explains simple tactics to make sure the financing process stays relatively pleasant, painless, and doesn't morph into a nightmare.

Chapter ten, **STARTING:** TURNING MY IDEA INTO MY COMPANY, summarizes many essential points in the book. As importantly, it tells you what you need to do to get your company up and running.

Right now, in your hands, is the key to taking that first step to come up with and/or transform a business idea into a venture that will provide you with more than you ever thought possible. The book shows you how to surmount most challenges, so you start off on the right foot and continue that way. But there is one big challenge left – YOU. All you need to do to overcome that is read on and ACT on the strategies in this book.

You should read this book actively. Read it a few times and have a pencil and paper out to take notes to capture the important points. Have these notes in front of you as you refine your business idea. So now, let's move on together and take the first step to achieving large profits, loving your work and having a life outside of your business.

Visit my website at **thebalancedentrepreneur.com** for more entrepreneurship information, startup tips, and marketing advice that will help you grow your successful business and live a great life.

• • •

"Finding my idea"

PART

# FINDING MY IDEA

• • •

# CHAPTER

# PERSONAL GOALS:
## Loving My Life As "The Boss"

• • •

**Outdated Strategy:**

Primarily focus early planning on making sure the business idea is financially viable.

**New "Balanced Entrepreneur" Strategy 1:**

Focus your early planning on making sure your idea will lead to enjoying the business and having a life outside of the business and being financially successful.

• • •

Don't get me wrong, I like money. I'm sure you like money. Let's build a business that makes money. It is true that there are steps you can take to shape your venture idea that will radically increase the amount of money you will make; steps this book will teach you.

But entrepreneurs don't just start a business to make more money. Achieving solid financial performance is just one part of achieving success. True venture success involves much, much more than this. In fact, in general, achieving high earnings is not even the most important outcome entrepreneurs want from their business. According to the study captured below, the four primary outcomes entrepreneurs desire are freedom to do things their own way, control of their time, security, and flexibility for a family and personal life. Having high earnings doesn't show up until outcome number five, well after the first four reasons.

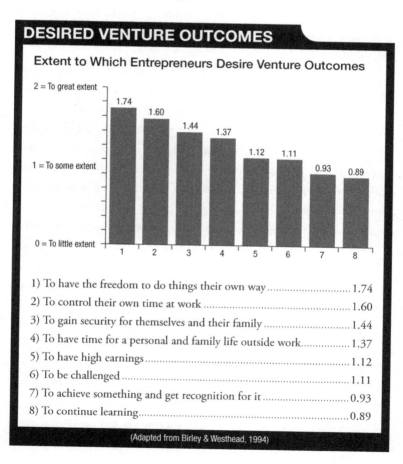

## DESIRED VENTURE OUTCOMES

### Extent to Which Entrepreneurs Desire Venture Outcomes

1) To have the freedom to do things their own way ............................. 1.74
2) To control their own time at work ..................................................... 1.60
3) To gain security for themselves and their family ............................ 1.44
4) To have time for a personal and family life outside work ............... 1.37
5) To have high earnings ...................................................................... 1.12
6) To be challenged .............................................................................. 1.11
7) To achieve something and get recognition for it ............................. 0.93
8) To continue learning ........................................................................ 0.89

(Adapted from Birley & Westhead, 1994)

19

Although initially one may be surprised by these results, after stopping to think about it, the findings make a lot of sense. Entrepreneurs often start a company to escape from a domineering boss who constantly tells them what to do and when to do it. After being thwarted for years, it is only natural that new venture founders want to do things their own way and to control their own time. Furthermore, it is logical that entrepreneurs now seek security from their ventures, given that corporate America's knee jerk response to any problem has become "lay off the employees."

Finally, entrepreneurs may start a venture to get more of a life outside of work, because of the long hours established companies demand. A survey by Expedia.com revealed that over 60 percent of Americans spend more than 40 hours at work and over 40 percent spend more than 50 hours. And that doesn't include the joys of commuting time. Furthermore, United States citizens often forgo the vacation time their company "owes" them and on average spend three weeks more at work per year than their western European counterparts. Even when U.S. employees are able to set aside what little time they have for themselves or family, they are probably too exhausted and stressed to enjoy it anyway.

Unfortunately though, way too many entrepreneurs are **needlessly** jumping out of the frying pan into the fire. These driven and passionate people often end up more of a slave to their own business than they ever were to their boss. Although they are "in charge", customers, employees or even the government dictate how they have to do things and by when they need to do them. Furthermore, they are so busy putting out fires and overseeing so many aspects of the company that they never get to do the tasks they really enjoy.

Ironically, while many entrepreneurs may have started their business because the corporate world provides less and less job security every year, many are far worse off as entrepreneurs. Not only are the entrepreneurs' future incomes often more precarious than ever, more problematically, they have frequently invested their entire savings and risk losing their home. Even more of a joke is their wish for time outside of the business. Frequently their only choice is which 25 hours a day they wish to work.

## Real Life Example – My Import Business

Throughout this book I will share examples with you to illustrate concepts. I think the examples are useful because they help you understand the ideas and how they relate to real life situations. I use examples as case histories when I teach my students.

My first example, appropriately enough, relates to my first business. Unfortunately, it illustrates how I learned by experience that ventures often don't achieve the results you want. When I was 18 years old, and my brother was just 23, we started a wholesale import company that sold gift and decorative accessories, like wall hangings. But I didn't know then what I know now – and I gave no thought to making sure the venture idea would generate the type of life I wanted.

Even at a young age I wanted to be an entrepreneur. After all, being an entrepreneur automatically meant I got be the boss, doing things my own way, when I wanted to do them. Right? No, Wrong. I never had time and was always reacting. I was constantly playing catch up; purchasing supplies, tracking shipments, counting inventory and of course hiring, firing and training employees.

Even when I tried to set aside time to do those things I liked in the business, the unexpected occurred. Packages were not getting

through customs, indispensable employees were unexpectedly quitting, special requests were made by customers, equipment breaking – you get the point. I constantly put out fires – once literally. Freedom to do things my own way and control my time – you have to be kidding me.

As the business progressed, my brother and I ended up putting in every last penny we had. And we still ran out of cash – so we tried to get a loan. The catch was, the only way the bank would give it was to have my parents cosign it, using their house as collateral. Made for some interesting holiday conversations.

As you may have guessed, our personal life was nil. My brother ended up breaking up with his long time girlfriend and my romantic life was non-existent. But who needed to date when they had carved Peruvian gourds they could be packing? Eighty hour weeks and seven day work weeks were the norm. And so far as we were concerned, the word "vacation" wasn't even in the dictionary – after all, my parents could lose their house if we failed.

## The Good News

The good news is that none of this was necessary. We could have avoided the lack of freedom, the huge risks, and the total absence of a life outside of the business. And we would have made far more money. **Before we started,** all we had to do was check our basic idea against certain criteria and refine it based on some simple strategies.

I know this to be true because, after a couple of years into the import business, we decided we were sick of struggling. So we started figuring out and incorporating some strategies in this book. We began to regain control of our lives, work sane hours, and all while growing the business quicker than ever. Ultimately we sold it for a lot of money. Too bad it took two years of misery before we got our better life. But you don't need to waste two years; you can start enjoying your business and life from day one by reading this book.

Even after life got to be quite good in our wholesale company, it was nothing compared to the pure joy I developed in later ventures after I accumulated more strategies and refined those I already learned. Take, for example, my wilderness canoe trip business. I worked four months lining up clients and preparing for trips and about three months "working" during the trips. I put working in quotes because my staff handled absolutely every single responsibility ranging from packing gear, to handling client needs, to buying equipment. Me – I canoed in some of the most pristine lakes and rivers in Canada, fished, and when I felt like it – which was pretty often – cooked over an open fire. Oh, and I also saw some of the most scenic sunrises and sunsets you could imagine. Not too arduous for a business which required an investment of less than $500 and made a huge profit almost from day one. In fact, it provided me with an affluent lifestyle and, not even counting the time I spent on the canoe trips, five months of vacation every year.

You may or may not be into canoeing, but you too can build a venture that permits you to live the life of your dreams. Maybe it's traveling to exotic locations, or perhaps spending time playing with toys – sports cars, boats, and maybe a private jet. Or perhaps it's just making sure you can be home by two thirty every day to talk to your children about what they did at school that day. As importantly, you can make sure that you look forward to going to the office everyday because you know you will be doing exactly what you want, and how you want to do it – whether it is cooking over a campfire, designing ads, or running karate classes. Because you've been doing what you enjoy, you can leave work each day filled with energy and ready to make the most of your free time. And oh yes, did I mention having money – lots of it.

But to achieve these things you need to concentrate on more than just making money at the outset. You need to spend as much effort on making sure your venture idea is consistent with enjoying each workday and having free time. That only makes sense, yet almost no one does it.

But which is likely to make you **more** money?

A. Planning a business that allows you to have a great life and wealth, or
B. Just focusing on wealth.

The surprising answer is **CHOICE A:** Planning a business that allows you to have a great life and wealth will lead to more money. Let me explain. While there are many factors that lead to financial success, people neglect the most important one. Nope, it does not relate to your product, market, service or company. All those are important, but not the most important thing. The factor that is most likely to lead to financial success is YOU being at your best. You must be enthusiastic, persistent, energetic, and on the ball. But you will only be at your best if you enjoy what you are doing, have a life outside of your company, and are relaxed because you haven't had to hock your house. Thus, becoming a balanced entrepreneur doesn't hinder financial success, it increases it.

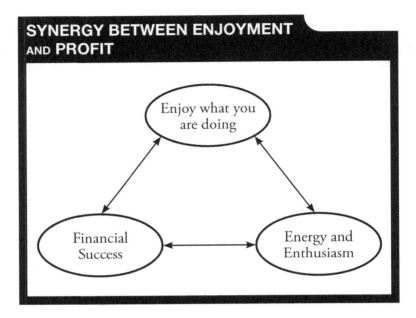

**SYNERGY BETWEEN ENJOYMENT AND PROFIT**

It starts a reinforcing cycle of achievement: the more you enjoy what you are doing, the more energy and enthusiasm you will have. The more energy and enthusiasm you have, the more financial success will you have. The more financial success you have, the more you will enjoy what you are doing. Is there more to it ... sure. But the fundamental logic holds. It is ultimately that simple.

This book will tell you exactly what you need to consider to shape your idea so that it can lead to a profitable, enjoyable business that doesn't overwhelm your personal and family life. But first, the next chapter explains a major common misconception of entrepreneurs that you must avoid to have a chance at the type of life you desire.

• • •

# CHAPTER SUMMARY

1. Don't **just** focus your idea on a venture's financial success.

2. Spend as much time focusing on making sure the idea will let you enjoy what you are doing and generate the time needed to have a life outside the venture.

● ● ●

Go to **TheBalancedEntrepreneur.com** for exercises, research and readings related to defining and achieving your personal goals.

Just click on the tab labeled "Resources".

CHAPTER

2

# THE IDEA:
## Finding It

• • •

**Outdated Strategy:**
Wait for the inspiration that leads to a great idea.

**New "Balanced Entrepreneur" Strategy 2:**
Systematically generate rough ideas and then perfect them.

• • •

The outdated strategy above represents a poor approach to coming up with a venture idea for two reasons. First and most simply, why wait when there are many things you can do to speed the process along, as this chapter will illustrate. Second, "perfect" or for that matter even "good" ideas don't just pop into your head fully grown.

Many potential entrepreneurs don't have an idea upon which to base their business. They believe it is hard to come up with an idea. They are wrong. Usually there are ideas all around them and they may have even considered many of them. What they haven't done is come up with an idea that is fully worked out and that they are confident will succeed. Bottom line, nobody can do this. Yet they let this be a barrier. That is why I wrote this book.

Instead I will show you a different, far better, approach. This chapter will illustrate how to derive a stream of ideas, far more than you could ever follow through on. The rest of the book will provide step by step instructions on how to perfect your idea, so your business will provide you with the life you want.

## FIVE SOURCES OF VENTURE IDEAS

New venture ideas are all around us. After identifying different sources of ideas, I will carefully explain how you can take advantage of the benefits and avoid the traps associated with each source. Finally, and perhaps most importantly, I prescribe actions you can take TODAY to radically increase the probability of generating ideas from that source.

### SOURCE #1: WORK EXPERIENCE.

Your past or current employment can provide a wealth of new venture ideas. In fact, I often rely on this resource for my own business ideas. My wilderness trips serve as a case in point. When I was a teen, I spent all my summers working for a teacher who ran summer canoe trips. Many years later, I decided to start my own wilderness business.

In addition, this book, and the knowledge-based products that will follow, all stem from my employment. For decades, I've started my own companies, taught entrepreneurship in universities and coached over a thousand budding entrepreneurs. I have also published my own research on venture founders as well as studied the findings of others stemming from tens of thousands of new ventures.

My experience taught me there were proven general strategies that entrepreneurs could use to shape their ideas that would simultaneously improve the financial and non-financial benefits of their ventures. Yet no one is systematically teaching those strategies to entrepreneurs. Given the tragedy some entrepreneurs' lives turn into versus the joy they could be, this omission is almost a crime. Hence, the idea for this book was born.

Anyone can generate ideas from their jobs. Think about your current place of work and what customers and/or colleagues gripe about. Can you come up with an idea that helps solve their problem? The coworkers of a machinist in a large aviation firm constantly complained about a shortage of certain parts. So he started a home-based parts courier service. His first customer? His former employer.

*Advantages:* Identifying an idea based upon your work experience can provide you with many benefits. Perhaps first and foremost, it may turn one of the major challenges of starting a new venture into one of your major advantages. Namely, potential customers are often reluctant to purchase products from new ventures, because the companies lack a track record. If you, however, unquestionably have personal experience in an area, that might diminish concerns. For example, I had worked on dozens of different types of wilderness trips before starting my own wilderness trip business. Also my vast experience teaching, researching and practicing entrepreneurship explains how my newest venture, namely this book and related products, can provide proven principles.

As importantly, choosing a venture that is based upon work experience propels you up the learning curve. You can avoid many mistakes novices might make. When I started my canoe trip business, I already had years of personal experience and knew what to expect.

I had, in my past, worked for someone else on every single aspect of running a wilderness trip business. Nothing caught me by surprise. The result: profits and sales increased smoothly and steadily.

In contrast, while it was true my brother and I made a success of our first business, the import company, the going was tough. In our early months, for example, we made the rookie mistake of taking on many untrustworthy clients, extending credit to far too many questionable accounts and not collecting funds aggressively enough. The result – we had to make yet another trip to the bank to beg for yet another loan. If we had more industry experience, we would have avoided this huge and potentially deadly blunder. The graphs below, although inexact, capture a major message about the sales and profit growth for both the canoe trip business and import company. While both were successful, I bet you can correctly guess which produced the more enjoyable, stress free lifestyle.

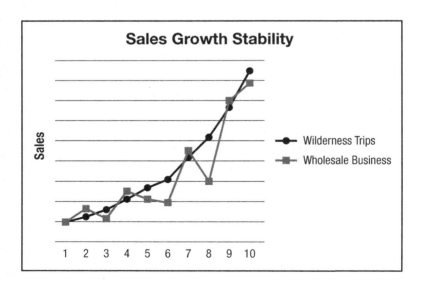

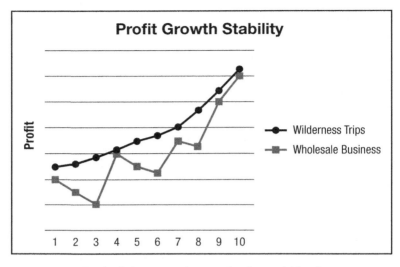

"Which business do you think would lead
to more enjoyment and less stress?"

Basing your venture on past work experience provides yet another benefit; it might lead to superior insights. Superior insights, in turn, can lead to superior profits, and, just as importantly, to a superior life.

My own work experience, for example, led to my current company and this book. Through my work, I learned:

1. many would-be entrepreneurs not only want their companies to be highly profitable, they also want to enjoy their work, and increase their freedom

2. few entrepreneurs attempt to shape their initial ideas to generate these other benefits

3. most struggle to achieve the financial benefits they seek and almost none obtain the non-financial benefits

4. entrepreneurs, in general, do not realize there ARE several strategies to perfect ideas so that they will generate BOTH the financial and non-financial benefits

5. these strategies are in scattered locations and often written in language that is difficult for entrepreneurs to translate and implement

Based on these insights gathered through my work, I knew this book and the products that follow can fill a real need.

*Dangers:* While basing your new venture ideas on your work experience spawns many advantages, it has its dangers. In particular, you will have to be very careful about conflicts of interest. If you have even a possible conflict of interest, you need to consult an attorney. Here are some of the issues you should be aware of:

1. Trade secrets: You cannot base your business on a trade secret. Trade secrets include formulas, devices or information used by one business to produce an advantage over competitors who don't have that particular knowledge.

2. Former employer's customers: You also need to be very wary about obtaining sales from your former employer's customers. In general, you cannot directly solicit them, but they are allowed to approach you. You also may make a very general announcement. Importantly, your employer usually cannot enforce an open ended non-compete agreement. Agreements must be limited as to time span and location.

3. Patents: You obviously cannot base your business on your employer's patented invention. However, if it is not patented and a reasonably skilled person could reverse engineer the invention from the finished product, you might be able to use it.

In my opinion, you should be completely up front with your employer. Try to leave on great terms and if possible, even get a written agreement stating what you can do. A fair and frank conversation might even lead your employer to become a strategic partner, a topic I discuss in Chapter 9. The machinist from the aviation firm I discussed earlier had a great start when his past employer became his first customer.

*Increasing the probability of generating ideas from your work experience:*

1. Work in an industry you want to enter. My canoe trip business serves as a case in point. Even though I started the business many years after I was initially employed in the industry, working in the business in my teens helped me enormously.

2. Convert your services into products. One popular way to generate a new business idea is to transform the current service you perform into a product. If, for example, you are a consultant, ask yourself whether there are techniques or tools you use that can be standardized and turned into books, audiotapes, videotapes, newsletters etc. A chief benefit of this approach is that you may be moving from a business model where you are paid in direct proportion to the hours you work, to one where you can make unlimited funds without increasing your hours. In other words, you are increasing the scalability of your business. This is key to starting the business that allows a great life; you can make more money, without increasing your workload.

3. Take notes of disagreements about how to proceed that occurred at companies you used to work for. Perhaps there are business opportunities in the paths not taken. Have you ever had an idea which was rejected? Frustrating, wasn't it? But it doesn't need to be. Turn that frustration into an opportunity.

Think about whether your rejected idea can form the basis for a business.

4. Every time you lose a sale, ask the customer why? If you can determine what needs your current company doesn't meet, you might identify an important unmet need.

5. Do school projects in industries of interest. If you are still a student, focus all your projects on an industry that interests you. You'd be amazed at the type of access to industry insiders and information people provide motivated students. Make sure to do a great job on the project. You could be talking to a potential partner or customer.

## SOURCE #2: HOBBIES.

Some people manage to turn their hobbies into businesses. In one sense I did this with my wilderness business. It was based on far more than just the canoe trips I had worked on. I participated in a wide variety of other outdoor experiences. These included multiple bicycle trips ranging from a hundred miles to a thousand miles, a winter cross country ski/camping trip where we faced temperatures between 30 below zero to 50 below zero, and an extended sailing trip with Outward Bound, one of the largest organizations that run wilderness expeditions.

Do you have a hobby or personal interest that could be turned into a business? Are you producing something someone else might want to buy? If yes, you might have a possible business. Take, for example, an individual who enjoyed cooking. He made a pretty great key lime pie, which all his friends said he should sell. He started part time, selling about 100 pies a week. Now his company turns out 1,500 pies a day and generates millions in revenue a year.

*Advantages:* Basing your business on a hobby has two potential benefits, both of which are huge. First, much like starting a business based on your work experience, starting a business based on your hobbies also suggests you may know what you are doing. You know the product, you know how to make it, and you know the type of people interested. What a great way to start.

Second, you presumably love what you are doing, or you would not be doing it for free. For the balanced entrepreneur, that is, a venture founder who looks forward to Mondays and enjoys waking up in the morning to go into work, this factor can make all the difference. For these two reasons alone, it is at least worth considering turning your hobby into a business.

*Dangers:* This is not to say that there are not potential pitfalls associated with starting a hobby-based business. Perhaps one of the greatest hazards is overestimating demand.

Sure, people have been raving about your creations for years, but small detail, were they just being polite?

Also, getting a compliment is easy, separating people from cash is a bit harder. Finally, when people view you as a hobbyist, they compare the product or service you produce to other amateurs, whereas when you are in business they only purchase when you are better than other professionals.

Even worse than overestimating demand based upon feedback from friends who are favorably predisposed, is overestimating demand because you are so close to the idea. You might project your wants and desires on others. This was certainly a potential danger when I decided to start a wilderness trip business. I love the outdoors – doesn't everyone? And canoeing is the best way to enjoy the outdoors – right? So clearly I could sign up 50 or 60% of the people I contacted. I had to remind myself that I was forming all my perceptions via my own eyes, those of someone who had spent every summer of his teen years canoeing.

There are many ways to make sure there is real demand out there, many of which I discuss in chapter six, when investigating marketing tactics.

One of the best ways to determine demand is to try to sell what you produce in a competitive setting very early on. Don't rely on your friends' opinions or even their purchases. Find some low cost way to see if unbiased people will actually purchase – maybe go to a flea market or place a small ad. A small trial can save you years of agony. Some early orders eliminate untold risks and hassles, making your life as an entrepreneur a dream. But you'll read much more on this tactic in chapter six.

Another way to get more objective feedback is to bring along a skeptical friend when interviewing potential customers. Rather than relying solely on your own interpretation of the interviewee's comments, ask your friend his or her version of what was said. This will help you avoid hearing only what you want to hear.

Also, have people that you survey "rank order" preferences and ideas, rather than just rating how much they like an idea. For example, when pursuing my canoe trip business, I did not ask people to respond to a statement like the following:

*"My child would be likely to go on a canoe trip this Summer."*

| 1 | 2 | 3 | 4 | 5 |
|---|---|---|---|---|
| Strongly Disagree | Disagree | Neither Agree nor Disagree | Agree | Strongly Agree |

Regardless of the business you are asking about, far too many respondents often give too positive a response. Instead, without telling the respondent which activity I was promoting, I asked them to "rank order" (i.e. rank in order of preference, beginning with 1 for their first preference) several summer activities that their child might participate in. Some of the activities might be:

_____ Going to a sports camp
_____ Participating in a wilderness canoe trip
_____ Working at a job
_____ Staying home
_____ None of the above

The technique above will give you a much better feel for people's real interests and desires.

Another major danger to avoid is running your business like it's still a hobby. You no longer can just work when you feel like it. You have customers who are counting on you. You also can't just do what satisfies you – you have to listen to your customers. You might like making eighteen inch wood carvings, but if the market is demanding them in twelve inches, guess what – you need to start making more twelve inchers.

Along a related line, being in business is not the same as practicing your craft. You have accounting, marketing and, god forbid, even possibly managing people to worry about. As I emphasize in chapter seven, think long and hard about which activities will take up your time and how much you enjoy those activities. If the scales are tipping towards too many activities you don't like, consider partnering up with someone.

### *Increasing the probability of generating ideas from your hobbies.*
Not meaning to be too obvious, the first step is to examine your hobbies. But do not define the term "hobbies" too narrowly. A "hobby" can be almost any activity in which you have an interest:

cooking, canoeing, hiking, painting, martial arts, sewing, you name it. Remember too, that you have two distinct paths you can take to build a business related to your hobby. The first route involves hobbies that generate output that can be sold. So sell it.

But what of the many hobbies that don't generate a salable output. There is still a potentially viable path to a business that you can pursue. Namely, assist others pursuing the same hobby. You can, for example, form a membership website or teach classes related to your hobby. You know what the interests of the participants would be, what tools they may need, and might have superior knowledge about the hobby. What a great place to start.

## SOURCE #3: TRENDS.

Many ideas for new ventures can emerge from trends. And like no other time in history, new trends that can fundamentally influence society are springing up. To mention just a few:

1. the number of senior citizens is unprecedented and continuing to grow,
2. information is spreading across the planet at unparalleled speeds,
3. people are connecting via the social web,
4. consumers are acknowledging the value of alternative medicine,
5. households are consuming organic foods,
6. individuals are paying higher energy costs, and
7. employees are working from home.

Dozens or even hundreds of new business ideas can be based upon any of the trends listed above or upon any of the thousands of other trends not listed. A record number of entrepreneurs, for example, started new consulting firms to help clients comply with the Sarbanes-Oxley Act of 2002 (corporate accounting and auditing reform). Additionally, entrepreneurs associated with medical and personal care have set up shop to capitalize on the needs of an aging population.

Perhaps, though, the trend which might result in more new venture ideas than any other is the desire to be green. An almost $800 billion federal stimulus bill may intensify the effects of this trend even further by freeing up funds for a wide variety of green initiatives. And the sheer diversity of the environmentally friendly endeavors inspires awe. While one entrepreneur, Riggs Eckelberry, started Origin Oil, which promotes the use of algae for fuel, another entrepreneur, Arnold Klans, formed BlueFire Ethanol to replicate Doctor Emmett Brown's achievement in the film "Back to the Future 2", namely to use garbage as an energy source.

Environmentally friendly business ideas are not limited to sources of fuel. They also span types of vehicles, including the first freeway-legal electric motorcycle in the world, as well as electric powered jet skis that may use a solar lily pad to recharge. But the green scene has extended far beyond vehicles, with entrepreneurs in a wide variety of industries seeking to differentiate their ideas by being ecofriendly. Take TS Designs, a company that dyes and prints T-shirts. This company decided to infuse a cornerstone entrepreneurial industry with the green phenomena. It uses water based inks on its shirts, employs alternative energies for its plant's power, and produces biodiesel on site to fuel the company truck.

*Advantages:* Ideas that piggy back on major trends can provide entrepreneurs with some major benefits. Since trends by their very nature imply change, they often create new opportunities for entrepreneurs. Furthermore, trends may create situations where demand for certain services and products exceeds the supply of those services and products. This, in turn, can translate into unusually high profits.

Also, you can often objectively verify trends. For example, we know with certainty that the proportion of seniors is growing. An entrepreneur who has a new venture idea that requires a growing number of senior citizens can proceed based on an objective fact, rather than on a subjective hunch.

*Dangers:* Like any of the sources of venture ideas, basing a business on a trend is not without potential dangers. First, while as just stated, trends can often be objective, one can also mistake fads for trends. By the time the entrepreneur gets his or her business up and running, the fad it is based upon might have already disappeared.

Problematically, basing your business on an objectively verifiable trend with staying power can also get you in trouble. Because the trend is so certain, before you know it you might have more competition than you anticipated or can cope with. While demand might have exceeded supply when you first formed your business idea, the gap might rapidly vanish, and with it, your chance of abnormally high profits. Fortunately, a solution to this problem is in the very next section.

### Increasing the probability of generating ideas from trends:

So just how do you generate an idea from a trend that is fairly certain to occur, yet not have everybody else jump on board? You have to act quickly and notice the trend before others. Of course that might be easier said than done, so let's include some additional tips that will let you identify trends all the sooner.

1. Observe. Watch TV, listen to people and read a wide variety of content from diverse sources including newspapers, magazines, political statements, blogs and tweets. What search terms are popping up on Google and Yahoo? But most importantly, do

all this with a laser focus on noticing new trends, and seek out diverse material from different sources. Always be searching.

2. Focus on leading indicators of trends. Pay attention to the east and west coasts, where fundamental changes so frequently start. Also, listen to the younger generation, as they often notice what is up and coming.

3. Develop a framework. The whole trick to starting your search for a new venture idea involves initially noticing as many trends as possible, as quickly as possible – before other entrepreneurs. Using a systematic framework might help you identify some trends you may have otherwise missed. Consider trends associated with the six categories below and see if you get any ideas for new ventures.

   a. Political
   b. Environmental
   c. Socio-cultural
   d. Technological
   e. Economical
   f. Legal

4. Probe deeper than the most obvious ramifications of the trend. One key to coming up with an idea that others won't notice is to thoroughly explore all the implications of the trends, not just the ones that most would observe. The demand for yoga, for example, is growing at an unprecedented rate. Clearly that creates the need for yoga classes, so you should start yoga classes, right? Not so fast. Unfortunately, the number yoga classes has rapidly increased to meet the demand.

Instead, like Jennifer McKinley and her partner Doreen Hing, you need to look deeper at the trend. Once you have identified a trend, identify all the needs it might create, not just the most obvious ones.

In addition to being active yogis, McKinley, 41, and partner Doreen Hing, 39, determined that practitioners of yoga wanted to express their individuality and wanted to explore different types of classes. This led the partners to offer specialized, unique classes, ranging from hot yoga (done in a heated room) to naked yoga (yep, you interpreted that correctly). Actually, most of their sales came not from classes but from offering a complementary product, namely chic, high end yoga mats. The mats allow for mass produced art imaging and contain a special traction surface layer ideal for practicing yoga. The result – a multimillion dollar business.

Also, ask if the trend might provide you with any additional capabilities that others may overlook. Many in the late 1990s predicted that DVDs would dominate the movie rental market. In contrast to VHS, DVDs allowed for subtitles, were more durable, and easily let viewers find out more about the movie they viewed. Not surprisingly, given these advantages, virtually all video stores started stocking them. But DVDs had one other benefit that all but one company initially overlooked. They could be mailed inexpensively. Only Netflix recognized this early on, an insight that will lead to over one and a half billion dollars in revenue and over one hundred million dollars net income in 2010.

## SOURCE #4: DISCONTENTMENT.

Reed Hastings, the founder of Netflix, didn't just start the company because he noticed a trend. He started it because he was furious after once again paying a late fee on a rental – this time $40. But why get mad when you can launch a new venture? Frustration, exasperation and anger has caused many a founder to take action to solve a personal problem. A lawyer, Elmer Winters, couldn't finish a legal brief in time because his secretary was out sick. Next thing you know he started a venture that would provide temporary clerical support called Manpower. In 2008, the company exceeded twenty billion dollars in sales.

*Advantages:* Developing a business idea that will alleviate your own discontentment can be a great way to go. Ideas stemming from personal dissatisfaction have many advantages, but one benefit probably outweighs the rest. Your business idea might help fill a real need experienced by many. If something creates negative emotion within you, that same thing probably bothers others as well – you just need to find them and present your solution.

Furthermore, you often may have a deep understanding of the problem. Debra Myers suffered from eczema, a chronic skin disorder that involves scaly and itchy rashes. One difficulty she faced was that standard bath and body products further irritated her already problematic skin. Using her kitchen blender, she began to experiment, trying to create non-irritating products from cocoa butter and shea butter (a yellowish or ivory-colored fat removed from the fruit of the shea tree). Ultimately, she came up with a solution that she and other sufferers she knew loved. Since she had personally experienced the problem, she knew the value of the solution.

*Dangers:* But Myers fared better than many. Many times, a source of discontent is not easily removed – something an entrepreneur may only find out after years of trying. If it had been easy, possibly others would have already found a solution. There are, however, two steps you can take to avoid spinning your wheels endlessly. First, explore whether anyone else has worked on, or is working on, this problem. If so, how did they fare? What different approach can you try? Second, at the outset, set firm milestones. What do you need to accomplish? By when? Also set limits on the resources that you are willing to expend.

*Increasing the probability of generating ideas from discontentment:* From now on, note what frustrates you. Also watch others more closely and listen to them carefully when they recite their problems. Take for example one student, Sawyer Sparks, who was taking an entrepreneurship class. He decided he would look close by in search of an obstacle he could help people overcome. He soon discovered that his professor suffered from celiac disease, that is, an intolerance to gluten, a protein found in wheat. But wheat is in beer products – uh oh – a dire problem. A significant percentage of people could not have a beer. They might be forced to have wine, or heaven forbid, end up not consuming any alcohol at all.

As serious as that was, though, Sawyer actually ended up with a focus even more touching. Millions of children with celiac disease could not join their peers using modeling clay (e.g., Play Dough) because the product is wheat based. Sawyer came to the rescue, though, finding a way to make it out of soy and building a company around the process.

As a result of his empathy, Play Dough offered $500,000 to buy the whole company, even though it was still operating out of Sawyer's kitchen. But things really got exciting when he turned down that offer and went on the TV show Shark Tank. In the show, five self made millionaires (i.e., the sharks) decide whether to invest in an entrepreneur's business. The sharks reject most outright, often dismissing the entrepreneurs with phrases like "get out of here;" "you're wasting our time;" and "that is the stupidest idea I've ever heard." From the few entrepreneurs who survive the process, the investors usually demand about double the ownership percent before investing.

Sawyer Sparks faced a far different scenario. Three of the sharks got into a bidding war to get in on his deal. Finally the investors partnered up, offering $300,000 for 51% of the company, instead of the $125,000 for 25% of the business that Sawyer wanted. In an almost unprecedented move, the sharks placed a higher value on the company than the entrepreneur. And for the first time ever, one of the investors virtually begged an entrepreneur to be a part of the deal. This episode shows the power of helping others overcome their discontent. In addition to coming up with a great venture idea, you might become a better friend or person in the process.

For the rest of your life, seeing or feeling discontentment can be a good thing. After perceiving it, spend some time thinking about how that frustration can be avoided, eliminated, or minimized. Be creative, asking many questions. You could end up with a great business.

## SOURCE #5: TRANSFER SUCCESSFUL IDEAS.

The final way to derive an idea is to transfer it from another area. This occurs in many different forms: you can transplant ideas from another industry, from another market segment, or from another location. While Tia Wou may have started Tote Le Monde, a handbag manufacturer, in New York, the seed for the business was planted on another continent. When Wou traveled to Bolivia, South America for a friend's wedding, she noticed the country's unique rich textiles. She believed these fabrics would appeal to the U.S. market, and Tote Le Monde was born.

While Tia used a tangible resource from another area, Todd Woloson was inspired by a custom. When visiting France, he decided to do as the French do, and mixed sparkling water with juices. Upon returning to the states he could not find a healthy bottled fruit drink that had a fizz, so he started Izze Beverage Co. to fill the gap.

You might also adapt practices from other industries to form the essence of your company. In fact, many are quite shocked to find out how Ford Motor Company's idea to use an assembly line arose. A Ford employee, William "Pa" Klann, introduced it after seeing something similar while visiting a Chicago business. Which one, you ask? A slaughterhouse, where he viewed a "disassembly line" on which animals were butchered as they moved along a conveyor. He was impressed by the efficiency of one person removing the same piece over and over and felt that cars could be built inexpensively by basically reversing the process.

Of course, ideas from other industries don't have to be quite so dramatic. For example, Vernon Hill, the owner of The Commerce Bank, incorporated his insights from previously running Burger King franchises to the banking industry, extending the banks' opening hours and providing other fast food type services.

*Advantages:* Transferring ideas may produce at least two major benefits to entrepreneurs. They can make sure the idea is unique, that is, that no one else is doing it in his or her area, be it an industry, geographic location or even a customer group. Thus, they may have no direct competition.

Perhaps more importantly, even though they might not face rivals, entrepreneurs will be using a proven model that works – at least somewhere. This is a unique combination and one that can be hard to beat. In fact, since you are practicing the idea in a unique area, you might even be able to be coached by the executives who originally executed the concept. It is truly astonishing how willing so many are to help you if you are not directly competing with them.

One entrepreneur noticed the dearth of book stores in her town and believed that opening one represented an opportunity. To learn about the industry, she called many other bookstore owners around the country. Most offered advice, and one invited her to work with him for two weeks, during which time he shared everything he knew about starting and managing the bookstore.

*Dangers:* Transferring a successful idea from another area is not without its potential pitfalls. One, however, outweighs all the rest, namely that there is something systematically different about the area to which you are transferring the idea. Don't try to open a winter ski resort in Florida. First, identify the underlying conditions that make the business successful in its current domain. Second, ask whether those conditions will exist in the area where you plan to practice the idea. You need to really know the demographics and needs of your particular market. Do local conditions truly fit the opportunity?

Woloson, the founder of Izze, believed trends in the United States would support sales of his beverage. He saw a hole in the beverage business. There just were not healthy soft drinks using real fruit juices, even though the natural foods market was growing rapidly and the sugar-laden sodas market shrinking. He was right – Izze's annual revenues are in the seven figures.

***Increasing the probability of transferring successful ideas:*** One's ability to successfully generate ideas by examining what others have done is, in large part, a direct function of effort and systematic search. There are many ways of going about it:

1. One of the first areas to focus on is the tried and true. Search for standard products or services that are in many areas but that your community doesn't have. If you cannot think of a concrete reason for the omission, you might just have uncovered the type of market imperfection that leads to very successful businesses. You can also try the reverse; are there businesses that serve your community that are missing elsewhere? If so, might you consider relocating? Just about every town can support basic products and services such as dry cleaning, ice cream shops, and convenience stores.

   Regardless of whether you are looking for unmet needs in your town or in other locations, there is a very convenient way to start to conduct research. All you need to do is use the yellow pages or a similar search engine to locate offerings in different areas.

2. Focus on trend leaders. New types of businesses tend to arise disproportionately in certain locations, for example, New York and California. So pay attention to those areas. If something new arises there that looks good to you, think about emulating it.

3. Read business publications. What new businesses are magazines and newspapers like *Fortune, The Wall Street Journal, Inc.,* and *Entrepreneur* featuring? Any you might like to start? The fact that someone has already done it is not a reason why you shouldn't start it. If it is in another area, it might be a reason why you should.

4. Study diverse settings. Don't just look in your area. Read about and talk to people from a broad range of industries, countries and groups. This diverse information might provide many gems that you can mine and move to your own setting.

5. Travel. One suggestion closely related to the one above is... travel. Traveling exposes you to new sights, people, places and practices. As importantly, your more relaxed state and pace often opens the floodgates for new ideas. Plus it's fun. What a great combination.

## WHAT NOW?

Hopefully you have been taking notes as you have read this. Have any ideas for ventures come to mind? If so, write them down. Even if you can't think of anything yet, write down some steps you will take to get them. Peruse business publications, carry around a notebook to record times when you or your associates are discontent, and record your hobbies. GET STARTED! NOW!

Don't worry yet whether or not your ideas are good. Don't start the screening process yet – at least one idea will be good by the time you're done with this book. I will be giving you many tools which you can use to eliminate poor ideas, or to transform poor ideas into ones which can generate wealth and more importantly allow for a great life. Just read on!

• • •

## CHAPTER SUMMARY

### Major Ideas

This chapter showed you how to "find" business ideas, making the point that ideas don't arise fully blown. It discusses five sources of ideas as well as advantages and dangers associated with each source. As importantly, the chapter explains how to increase the likelihood of generating ideas from each source. The table below summarizes some of the information.

### Sources of Ideas

| Sources of Ideas | Advantage | Danger | Steps to Generate Ideas |
|---|---|---|---|
| **Work Experiences** | Have specialized knowledge | Might generate conflicts of interest | Explore reasons why company loses sales |
| **Hobbies** | Enjoying what you are doing | Running your business like a hobby | Examine assist-ing others exploring same hobby |

| Sources of Ideas | Advantage | Danger | Steps to Generate Ideas |
|---|---|---|---|
| Trends | Create situations where demand exceeds supply | Mistaking fads for trends | Probe deeper than the most obvious ramifications of the trend |
| Discontentment | Filling a real need | May not be able to resolve | Take note of the frustrations of yourself and others |
| Transfer successful ideas | Using a proven model | Underlying conditions may differ | Travel |

Keep in mind that none of the advantages or dangers are automatic. Fortunately, as the rest of the book explains, there are many more steps entrepreneurs can take to secure all the potential benefits of their ideas and avoid the potential dangers.

● ● ●

Go to **TheBalancedEntrepreneur.com**
for exercises, research and readings
related to finding ideas.

Just click on the tab labeled "Resources".

"Perfecting my idea"

# PART

**2**

# PERFECTING MY IDEA

• • •

### CHAPTER 3
COMPETING I:
Eliminating Low Profit, High Risk Ideas

### CHAPTER 4
COMPETING II:
Using Three Tactics To Increase
My Freedom And Wealth

### CHAPTER 5
THE INDUSTRY:
Avoiding Dangerous Traps

### CHAPTER 6
MARKETING:
Employing Techniques To Increase
My Free Time And Decrease My Costs

CHAPTER

# COMPETING I:
## Eliminating Low Profit, High Risk Ideas

• • •

**Outdated Strategy:**
Compete based on producing goods and services at a low cost, moving quickly, or being customer oriented.

**New "Balanced Entrepreneur" Strategy 3:**
Do not base your strategy on having a lower cost structure, greater speed, or higher customer satisfaction.

• • •

Counting on any one of these three things is a sure path to financial struggle, a miserable work life, and 80 plus hour work weeks. Unfortunately, I learned this one the hard way – from my experience with the import company. When we started, we figured we'd compete by having little overhead. Initially we operated out of my parents' basement. Rent was zero. Utilities were zero. We took as little out of the business as possible – often paying ourselves less than minimum wage or even nothing.

Slowly, we took over room after room of my parents' house, until my parents started finding Peruvian gourds in their bed. Finally, we had to move on, so we rented a warehouse to store inventory. We still wanted to keep our overhead low, so, to save on cooling and heating bills, we set the thermostat to 50 degrees in the winter, and never used air conditioning in the summer.

And guess where we slept? That's right, in the warehouse to save on rent. Our beds were literally made from cartons of wall hangings and gourds. Boxes served as our furniture.

I can't say we hated going into work, though. But only because we never left work — literally. In addition to living there, we easily worked over 90 hours a week. My brother and I worked together, ate together, and slept in the same room. I love him, but man did I get sick of him!

To top it all off, we still were not making money!

As mentioned, eventually we got it right and I never tried to compete again solely by keeping my business's overhead low. Good thing too, because I'm older now and my back would not do well if I slept on boxes of gourds every night.

So let's do a quick double check. Did we love what we were doing? No. Strike one. Did we have free time to live a life? Heck no. Strike two. Finally, did we generate a large profit? Absolutely not. Strike three. But striking out was predictable. Simply stated – our concept was fatally flawed.

## Established Firms Have the Advantage

We forgot – or didn't realize – a fundamental fact of entrepreneurship. All things being equal, established firms have the advantage over new startups. Period.

Yet entrepreneurs often believe the exact opposite. In fact, the very reason why many entrepreneurs are sure they will succeed is that they think their new ventures will be stronger than established firms. Their rationale for triumph is actually the cause of their future misery. These faulty reasons usually fall into one of four categories and I literally get a knot in my stomach when I hear an entrepreneur uttering them.

### Faulty Reason #1: We will have lower overhead cost.

The first faulty reason goes something like this: "I can be less expensive than the competition because I don't have overhead." This was a major rationale we used at the import company, and you saw how that worked out. The truth is, it costs new ventures more to conduct business than it costs established firms.

First, established firms achieve economies of scale (EOS) which lower their costs. EOS's occur when a company's per unit price drops because it is producing a large number of one type of item. Take, for example, an automobile manufacturer. Imagine that this company produces just one car a year. That one car will cost them millions of dollars. Alternatively, if they're making thousands of cars they can spread their costs over multiple units, including the huge costs associated with developing a new car model and the costs of building and running their assembly line. They can also make bulk purchases from suppliers.

Furthermore, established firms avoid all the expenses associated with starting from scratch, such as the cost of acquiring a new customer versus keeping an established customer. Simply stated – IT WON'T BE CHEAPER FOR THE NEW VENTURE – It's not going to happen.

But let's assume for just a moment that it could happen. You might still be thinking, "I'm not going to have a lot of overhead, I'm working out of the house, I'm willing to just pay myself minimum wage, I'll get relatives or friends to provide cheap or discounted services. That's how I'll compete."

What you've just told me is you have a fundamentally flawed business model. Your business can't get bigger without losing its advantage. Eventually, it would outgrow your house, you'd run out of friends and family to exploit, and one day you'd need a real salary. Poof, there goes the whole basis of your business's existence. Maybe your business could survive for a while on the basis of low overhead, but it would not thrive. As importantly, your life would be dreadful. Life's short, so enjoy what you do! Generate free time. Don't think you can compete based on low costs.

### Faulty Reason #2: We'll move quicker.

The second faulty reason relates to the entrepreneurs' belief that they will be able to move quite quickly. While this is sometimes true, there are many factors why, on a daily basis, new ventures might be slower to act than established firms.

For example, established firms are already skilled at tasks that new ventures are trying to learn from scratch. Think about the first time you ever tried bowling or golf. How long did it take you to master the skill?

Why do you think it will be so different when you or your staff, if any, act within your startup? How much effort will you need to get the very first product produced? How long will it take and how hard will it be to make a first sale versus just getting repeat orders like established companies do? Initially these "firsts" will go slowly and quite possibly turn out poorly. The time and effort can only be reduced after you've refined the process, repeating it over and over again.

Along a similar line, you won't have any policies established. Since initially, each situation will be new, you will have to take time out to make decisions. After a while, however, many of the decisions become automatic and subject to policy. Also, you may be very short of staff. This will obviously slow down any process.

Finally, it might take longer to perform certain tasks because you may not have the most efficient technology. Unlike your established counterparts, your company may not be able to justify the expense, because you can't spread the cost over enough units produced. So instead, you may be stuck with inefficient ways of doing things.

**Faulty Reason #3: We'll have higher customer satisfaction.**
Many entrepreneurs believe that they will succeed because their company will be more customer focused than larger firms. Unfortunately, that usually doesn't happen. Most small business owners are putting out so many fires that they often lose sight of the customer. They don't mean to, but at the end of an 80 hour work week, with suppliers, employees, and lenders creating problems for you – how patient do you think you will be?

Plus, unlike some larger firms who have people exclusively devoted to customer service, you will have fewer people doing a wider variety of tasks. This means that quite often, customers with a problem may not even be able to speak with an appropriate representative.

Finally, unlike their larger counterpart, new companies will not usually have the extra funds to invest in extensive market research to make sure policies and actions will please customers. Nor do they have extensive metrics that may relate to customer satisfaction, such as tracking ongoing customer attitudes, reorder rates, and average order size.

### Faulty Reason #4: The 2% rule.

Entrepreneurs frequently provide one other unjustifiable rationale for success. I refer to this rationale as "the 2% rule." I have heard so many entrepreneurs say something like, "Oh, all I need to do is capture 2% of this hundred million dollar market and I will get $2 million dollars in sales." But they never state a valid motive why on earth ANYONE should purchase from them. They have no reputation and are competing against other enterprises with years of experience.

Furthermore, even if the entrepreneur somehow does capture 2% – he is almost guaranteed a miserable life and likely bankruptcy. Why? Established firms, with all their cost advantages, often have net profit margins that are less than ten percent. Since new ventures will probably have costs that are over ten percent higher than established firms, they are likely to LOSE MONEY ON EVERY ITEM THEY SELL.

If it were so easy to profitably capture 2% of the market, then virtually every new venture would make it – since most markets are pretty large. The truth is, of course, that more ventures fail than succeed. It is irrefutable that, on average, established firms have higher profit margins, lower failure rates and more stable earnings than new ventures. Bottom line, they are stronger than small new ventures.

## An Analogy: Why Established Firms Win

In some ways the entrepreneur's belief that his or her tiny new startup can compete with large established competitors is the equivalent of a football team comprised of 12-year-olds believing they could score against an NFL team. Their competition is bigger and stronger. The average 12-year-old might weigh 130 pounds; the average professional football player 270 pounds. The NFL team has vast experience and has been running through plays hundreds of times. In fact, many of the players may have practiced together for years and know each other's moves like the back of their hand.

Like the 12-year-olds, if you try to compete against the big guys, you're going to end up bruised, battered and totally overwhelmed. It is a sure path to disliking your workday, putting in too many hours, and struggling financially.

The good news is that the next chapter discusses what you should do to avoid this outcome. In it, I share one general rule and three specific strategies that will let you build a venture that leads to superior financial performance and allows you to have a great life.

• • •

# CHAPTER SUMMARY

## Major Ideas

The central idea of this chapter is that often entrepreneurs erroneously believe that their ventures will be stronger than established firms in certain areas. In truth, established firms actually have the advantage in these areas. The following table summarizes the details.

| Advantages of Established Firms | Reasons |
|---|---|
| Able to produce goods/services at lower costs | 1. Costs spread over many units<br>2. Discounts for purchasing large volume<br>3. Avoids expenses associated with starting from scratch |
| Quicker | 1. Don't need to learn from scratch<br>2. Have established policies to respond to recurring situations<br>3. Have enough employees to deal with unexpected situations<br>4. May have more sophisticated equipment |
| Higher customer satisfaction | 1. Not as distracted by multi tasking and putting out fires<br>2. Have staff exclusively devoted to customer service<br>3. May have performed extensive research on customers wants |

CHAPTER

# COMPETING II:
## Using Three Tactics To Increase My Freedom And Wealth

• • •

**Outdated Strategy:**
Compete by taking customers from established competitors.

**New "Balanced Entrepreneur" Strategy 4:**
Avoid directly challenging established competitors. Instead, try getting new customers to enter the industry by serving an unfulfilled need, developing extraordinary skills, and/or entering markets where demand exceeds supply.

• • •

True success is not determined by how well you compete, but by how well you avoid competing. You need to shift your mental model. Don't ask yourself how you can be better than competitors; ask yourself how to have NO real competition. This not only produces a higher income business, but also will give you the freedom to enjoy your life.

Let's return to our analogy of the 12-year-olds trying to score against an NFL team. So, how could a team of tweens score touchdowns against a larger, stronger, and vastly more experienced NFL team?

Really think about it. How can it be done? Stumped?

All they need to do is go to an empty football field where the other team isn't. Run into that end zone to their heart's content and score touchdown after touchdown after touchdown.

Okay, you're probably thinking, "Wait a minute, Mark. No offense, but that idea is really stupid. The 12-year-olds may reach the end zone, but the points won't count. It's breaking a lot of rules. You can't just go to another football field where the team you're playing against isn't. Come on – get with the program."

And you know what – you're right. The idea of competing in football that way is extremely silly. But here's the beauty of the analogy. While it won't work for football, it will work for your new venture.

How can a new venture successfully compete against more established, larger competitors? The basic overall strategy it must follow is to avoid the competition. It must go to its own playing field.

Stop reading and write down in big bold letters...

# AVOID THE COMPETITION

Battling directly with competitors is just too tough a path. As mentioned in the previous chapter, competitors often can produce goods/services at a lower cost, move more quickly and are more customer oriented – all of which will make it difficult for you to generate a great living. And there are additional problems associated with direct competition. Potential buyers will compare your price to that of others, which cuts into your venture's profits and your ultimate wealth.

Plus, trying to steal someone away from a company is tough. Never underestimate the power of a customer's inertia and existing loyalties. And not surprisingly, other companies don't like it when you try to take their customers. They will battle fiercely to keep them. Bottom line, pursuing this strategy will force you to work long hours, always struggling to put in that much more effort than the competition. Your venture will be the boss of you, rather than you being the boss of it.

Instead, the path to greater freedom and fortune is to find new "unattached" customers and approach them with a unique offering. Bring new people into the market. Your prices will not be directly comparable to those of others, so your profits won't be limited. New customers will be easier to attract since they haven't already formed strong relationships. Furthermore, established companies may not fight for them, since the companies never had them in the first place. You will be in control and can win big, all while putting in shorter hours and less effort.

## Companies that Avoided the Competition

Many companies have sidestepped competition to minimize their struggle and become incredibly successful. One example that I just love is Heelys, the sneakers with the little rollers on the bottom. They allow you to walk anywhere but also let you skate. Nothing like Heelys existed. The company created its own market.

"Avoided the competition"

On a somewhat smaller scale, Detroit-based entrepreneur Tom Nardone's experience provides a detailed illustration of the freedom and success an entrepreneur may experience by avoiding direct competition. The name of his company is "PriveCo".

Never heard of it? Well, in some ways that's how Tom wants it; after all, the business's motto is "The world's most private company." The company sells products over the web that customers are embarrassed about purchasing. Before Tom, if you needed hemorrhoid ointment, you were likely to purchase it from the 16 year old cashier at the local pharmacy. In contrast, Priveco allows you to purchase your products confidentially. The company is all about protecting your anonymity. It never sends unsolicited emails or keeps mailing lists. In fact, the outside label on the package of any product you order only reads "PriveCo Inc.", giving no indication of what lies within.

When Tom founded the company, nothing like it existed – no competitors operated in the same way he did. Tom is quick to explain, "I wanted to find my unique space; competing against existing competitors is just too hard. You have to be perfect; you have to avoid mistakes. I'm not a perfect type of guy. I wanted to able to make errors and still do well." He goes on to flippantly state, "Hey, I'm lazy."

As a result of this philosophy, he's built a great business. He started it in 1998, while he was still in his 20s. Before he thought possible, it became a multimillion dollar enterprise and was one of the internet's fastest growing companies.

But it has done more for Tom than provide a great living; it's helped him build a great existence. He enjoys a fantastic family life with his wife and three children, travels all over the world to surf, does extensive volunteer work for multiple not-for-profits, often serving on their executive board, and has hobbies galore. For fun, he started attending art classes and holds an annual competition where people show what they can create using only one sheet of plywood.

But no discussion of Tom's hobbies would be complete without mentioning his passion for pumpkin carving. "I carve all through the season," Nardone said. Tired of boring pumpkins, he started creating pumpkins unlike any seen before. In his spare time, he has written a book on pumpkin carving which he has discussed on Regis and Kelly, Good Morning America and MTV. The book has sold out twice. The extremepumpkin.com website he built has received over a million hits. On it, he explains, "Carving pumpkins is something I enjoy ... I decided to make a pumpkin carving site that included shocking, funny, and gross pumpkin designs. The concept is about adults having fun. .... It is just a fun website that I put together."

Okay, but is pumpkin carving your thing, and are you interested in writing a book about it? And what if traveling around the world to surf isn't appealing to you? The answers to those questions don't matter. The point is, that by avoiding competition you won't have to execute your idea perfectly and have work dominate your life. Instead, you will have the time, freedom and money to spend your spare time on whatever your passion may be. For you, the goal may be spending more time with the family, going on camping trips, traveling around the world to relax in luxury resorts, joining a book club, or buying a vacation home – only you know for sure.

So you now know the overall strategy for achieving both financial success and for building a business that gives you the freedom to live a great life. The remainder of this chapter explains, in detail, how to avoid direct competition using three tactics, some of which may at times overlap. Applying more than one might even increase your benefits.

In addition, I will also explain the most common traps associated with each tactic and how you can steer clear of them.

## THREE TACTICS TO AVOID THE COMPETITION
**Tactic #1: Serve an unfulfilled need.**

The first way to avoid the competition is to introduce a product or service that addresses an unfulfilled need. Since nobody is currently filling the need, there is no competition.

One way to derive great ideas to serve an unfulfilled need is to utilize a unique space map. A unique space map illustrates two benefits or features that might fit together, that no one product in the industry to date has captured. Heelys serves as an example of a company that found a unique space in the footwear market. The figure on the next page portrays products in the footwear industry. It shows that dress shoes can be worn in some places but don't help you have fun. The figure also reveals that sneakers can be worn in many places and facilitate some fun activities, but they are still not the be all and end all in terms of providing a good time. Alternatively, ice skates and roller skates are a blast, but there are very few places you can use them. But look – way up on top of the graph on the right hand side of the map – Heelys. You can wear them in as many places as sneakers and have a great time doing so. Better yet, even though they combine two benefits, they are actually less expensive than many other types of footwear.

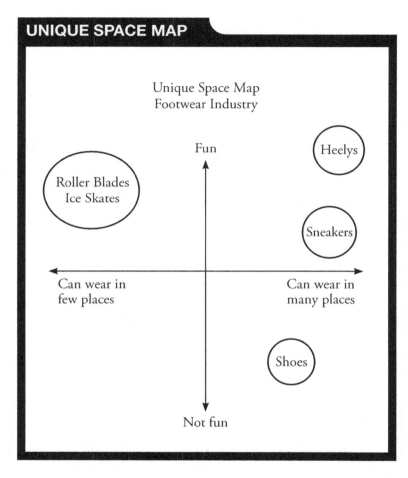

UNIQUE SPACE MAP

Unique Space Map
Footwear Industry

One interesting product that satisfied a previously unfulfilled need was on the TV show, The American Inventor. The product called "The Guardian Angel" is basically a scaled down sprinkler system with a sprinkler head shaped like an angel. The head goes on the top of a Christmas tree. If a Christmas tree ever catches fires, which happens somewhere every Christmas season, the Guardian Angel immediately goes off and helps extinguish the flame. Talk about unfulfilled needs. Without the Guardian Angel, Christmas tree fires might destroy homes and kill families. Nothing like the Guardian Angel was on the market and the product had no competitors.

Let's examine a company with which you may be more familiar. How did Wendy's succeed when the fast food industry already had firmly entrenched competitors? When Dave Thomas launched the chain, could he steer clear of the giants, McDonald's and Burger King? The two were in virtually every community in the country. Making matters worse, when Thomas opened his first Wendy's, industry sales were flat and the failure rate for new restaurants was through the roof.

Wendy's thrived by serving an unfulfilled need in order to avoid the competition. They targeted childless baby boomers. Before Wendy's, fast food restaurants focused on families and, more importantly, children. The Big Two had kids' meals and playgrounds. Nor is it a coincidence that McDonald's spokesperson is a clown – Ronald McDonald – and Burger King's "representative" is the magical, mystical Burger King, another icon aimed at children.

In contrast, adults wanted to eat bigger, juicier burgers in an attractive environment. Consequently, Wendy's was the first to offer higher quality food, larger portions, and an interesting décor. Clearly these were not tactics which would appeal to the families frequenting McDonald's or Burger King.

Importantly, Wendy's found it easy to convince their potential customers to give its products a try, since customers new to the market had no pre-existing loyalties. Furthermore, the two colossals in the industry, Burger King and McDonald's, were very slow to respond because they were not directly losing sales to Wendy's. The end result – before McDonald's and Burger King knew it, in record time Wendy's became the third biggest hamburger chain in the world.

*Avoiding Traps Relating To Serving An Unfulfilled Need.* Although starting a business based on serving an unfulfilled need can lead to success and a better life, there are a couple of traps you can fall into when you pursue this strategy.

*Make sure you are serving a real need.* The first trap entrepreneurs fall into is to believe there's a need when one doesn't exist. People think that anything different or "cool" serves a need – but that's often not the case. Ask yourself, "Are there real benefits to my product or service, and does anyone care about those benefits?"

Those of you with a technical background – engineers, for example – are most often victims of this trap. What you invent may be technologically sophisticated, elegant, and even brilliant. But, too frequently, no one other than you would care about all its extra features. Never forget that there's a customer out there and the job is to cater to his or her desires.

*Be sure you can really fill the need.* There is a second common trap entrepreneurs fall into when they base their venture on meeting a previously unmet need. They can't really fill the need even though it is real and important. Take, for example, the contestant on The American Inventor who designed a copper hat which he thought would keep people young. The seventy-year-old contestant wore it all the time and looked and acted like he was in his fifties. But I was skeptical that his youthful appearance stemmed from the hat. So were the judges who booted him off the show in record time. The need for the fountain of youth is about as basic and timeless as it gets. But did his hat really fill this need?

Even sophisticated, well educated individuals can fall prey to this mistake. I consulted with one group of doctors and high ranking administrators in the healthcare profession who wanted to develop a comprehensive medical advisory service. In part, they would teach their members to take preventative action in order to avoid illness. For example, they would get their members to be healthier by eating right and exercising regularly.

So I asked them, how were they going to get clients to improve their nutrition and to work out? They explained enthusiastically,

"Well at least once a month, maybe even more, we're going to send the members emails about healthy living. This way we will get them motivated to take care of themselves."

I wish it were that easy! If it were, I'd probably be a bodybuilder. But it's not and I'm not. My guess is that most people would immediately delete the email messages. And one just doesn't burn that many calories hitting the delete key. These potential entrepreneurs identified a great need but their company probably wouldn't be able to meet it.

### Tactic #2: Develop Extraordinary Skills.

The second way to avoid the competition is by developing such a strong skill that you set yourself totally apart from the competition. If your skills are far enough beyond your competitors, you are likely to attract a whole new clientele.

Your skill set must be so extraordinary that it will place the product or service in a class of its own. The key word here is **extraordinary**. If you are taking notes (and you should be) write the word down.

# Extraordinary

Let me share a real life example about a martial arts studio. First, I'm going to explain all the reasons why they had little or no chance of success. Then, I'm going to add a little twist to the story.

Two people had been taking karate for about a year and a half when their instructor tried to sell them a franchise. Neither one had business experience. Neither one of them was a good sales person. Neither one even had a black belt yet, and more alarmingly, even for their belt level, they weren't great martial artists.

The franchise had no brand identity and no name recognition. Even worse, the studio was going be located in a community which had plenty of martial art facilities already.

But the two potential entrepreneurs hated their current jobs. They were convinced, like so many others with a business idea, that starting a venture would be a path to a better life.

They ignored everyone's advice who told them to proceed cautiously. They often responded to legitimate concerns in a superficial or even naïve fashion. For example, they were warned that getting a lawyer to examine the franchise agreement would be expensive. Their counter; "It won't cost us anything. The franchise company is "so supportive" that it is going to provide its own lawyers free of charge." Don't get me wrong, the two were very intelligent, but when you really want something you can act in ways which aren't so sharp.

So they invested their life's savings to buy the franchise. Almost EVERY PENNY they had.

Guess how long it took them to go out of business? Five years, one year, six months, less? Whatever you would have said – I'll bet you were way, way off.

They never went out of business and were amazingly successful. They thrived from day one. Since starting over 20 years ago, they have been number one in sales in the whole franchise system, and are one of the most profitable studios in the country. They have almost a 50% market share in their area, even though there are six other studios in their immediate vicinity.

Why did they succeed? I said this story has an interesting little twist. I didn't give you some information. They had one extraordinary skill that was vital to their studio's success. The skill made up for the mistakes they made due to lack of experience. They didn't have to sweat every error or be perfect. In one sense, they had no competition because no other studio was remotely in their class.

Namely, they excelled at dealing with kids. And I do mean excelled. First of all, they were a husband and wife team, which automatically says family. They also had degrees in child psychology. In addition to being teachers in their earlier careers, they spent years working with children who were so emotionally disturbed they had to be placed in long term hospital care.

Between them, the couple supplemented this experience with being a juvenile probation officer, working at summer camps, and volunteering for childrens' charities. Given their vast experience, managing forty plus kids ranging in age from five to thirteen who were participating in a physical activity was a piece of cake.

Also important was how those skills compared to the competition. No offense to the instructor who taught me martial arts, but let me describe one of the techniques he used to "control" the kids who attended his classes. This is going to sound abusive, but it really wasn't. When a kid acted out in class, the owner had a set "routine" he delivered in a very heavy Korean accent that was often impossible for even adults to understand. He told the child "Hands against the wall." He would then command "Stick your butt out," as he grasped his seven foot long bamboo staff. In very slow motion he would swing it. As he thwacked the child on the butt, he would shout, "Willie Mays." Humorous yes – effective no.

In fact, children sometimes intentionally misbehaved to play a part in the "Willie Mays" skit that was "their punishment." This story represents my instructor's skill at dealing with children.

So you tell me if you think the married couple had extraordinary skills compared to their competition. As word spread about their ability to manage kids, they attracted many children with more than average behavior problems. The competition literally could not have handled the behavior problems of many of the children attending the couple's studio. The couple actually expanded the market, attracting many kids to martial arts who never would have participated otherwise.

For another example of a startup based on extraordinary skills, let's return to my first company, the import business. We went from barely keeping our doors open, sleeping on boxes, and working well over 80 hours a week to enjoying our workdays, gaining a life outside of the business, having money pour in and eventually selling the business for a substantial amount.

So what caused the transformation? Initially we competed just like every other small decorative accessory wholesaler. To cover the entire United States, we outsourced the sales function to multiple wholesaler representative companies. Each company had exclusive rights to several states, to sell our products and some non-competing items. We, like other small wholesalers, did not have a broad enough product line to justify traveling around the country selling goods.

We soon realized, however, that we were ignoring an extraordinary skill of my brother. Selling! Anything to anybody! But we had to tap into this skill, creatively. To make an initial purchase, store owners insisted on seeing and handling the goods. But as mentioned, my brother could not show our merchandise to mom and pop shops throughout the country. So what did we do? After the initial order, he telephoned each customer and convinced them to make large reorders.

Wholesaler representatives also bought booth space at annual trade shows, where they sold goods from all the companies they represented. Thousands of retailers from nearby states would attend. With our limited product line, it wasn't cost effective to purchase our own booths at trade shows. So instead, in exchange for granting representatives exclusive territories, we demanded the right to help man their booths. While there, we would handle our product sales. Finally, to convince national chains to buy, my brother went around the country visiting their buyers.

By relying on my brother's extraordinary selling skills, our reorders tripled and our gross sales at trade shows increased fivefold. Also, for the first time, department store chains started placing orders. Each purchase was usually more than our entire first year's revenue. These chains typically never purchased from small wholesalers, thus we increased the size of the market ordinarily available to small wholesalers.

*Avoiding Traps Relating to Extraordinary Skills.* Of course, there is not a magic potion for success, and entrepreneurs who believe they have extraordinary skills need to avoid the pitfalls listed below.

*Confirm that your skills really are extraordinary.* The biggest trap relating to extraordinary skills is believing you have an extraordinary skill when you do not. Are you sure your skills are extraordinary, or is it something you just tell yourself? Can you back up your opinion with concrete examples? Can you find several people, other than friends and relatives, who will verify your opinion of your skills?

Most importantly, are the skills extraordinary relative to the competition? Unfortunately, I cannot tell you how many people who want to open a restaurant say, "I'm going to be able to succeed because I'm a really good cook – after all, my friends and family rave about my food." That's it. That's their sole reason for believing that they can do well in one of the most competitive industries in the world.

Do they think the rest of the industry is comprised of restaurants where the head chefs can't boil water and are awful cooks? Sorry, but almost all head chefs can cook well. More often than not, entrepreneurs who tell me they will succeed because of their cooking ability are really telling me they are going to compete head to head against large and established competitors, and are more than likely going to struggle.

What of the claim I made that my brother had extraordinary selling skills in our import business? Can I back it up with **concrete** evidence or is it just my opinion? When he was 13 years old he won a nationwide sales contest selling greeting cards door to door. Not that many years later, he again broke all company sales records selling family portraits. Later, he earned enough by selling magazine subscriptions part-time to pay for his whole Ivy League college education and had tens of thousands of dollars left over to start the import business. He retired at forty-eight, having earned millions of dollars selling real estate. I could go on.

Remember, to avoid competition by depending on extraordinary skills, you must be so far above the competition that you are in a class of your own. It's rare, but as examples utilizing my brother and the martial arts studio illustrate, it happens.

***Explore whether the extraordinary skills are crucial.*** The other trap occurs when one has an extraordinary skill, but it's not a skill that matters. For the martial arts studio, ironically I would argue that maybe being the greatest martial arts fighter isn't a skill that matters to most of us. It doesn't mean you can teach.

Alternatively, and less obvious, being able to control kids is a skill that matters. Of course, even within the martial arts industry, you need to focus on the kids' market if excelling at childcare is what sets you apart.

You need to think carefully about your product and your customers, and ask yourself whether your extraordinary skills will really help produce a product or service that will generate cash.

## Tactic #3: Enter Markets where Demand Exceeds Supply.

The final method of avoiding direct competition is entering existing markets where demand exceeds supply. This allows you to escape head to head competition because you're not necessarily battling any other company for sales. To review ways to identify these markets, see the discussion of trends in chapter two.

An example from the entrepreneurship program for economically disadvantaged youth I ran comes to mind. The program loaned several groups of kids funds they used to purchase goods to sell at a flea market. Anything above the loan amount, they kept. The groups all went to the same store to buy their products, at the discount price we had prearranged.

Unfortunately, after getting to the flea market, the youngsters realized all the groups had chosen to sell the same products. Thus, most had to charge very low prices, and ultimately sold little. Instead of getting discouraged, though, one group got off their butt and found the solution. And when I said got off their butt, I meant it. They sold the fold-up chairs they were sitting on. It was a product no one else was selling and many people wanted, including other merchants at the flea market. Being the only ones selling their chairs, the team charged a high price, and at the end of the day earned eight times as much as any of the other groups. Plus they sold out of chairs early; and having made a great profit, took the rest of the day off to enjoy the flea market and buy themselves gifts with some of their profits. In other words, they achieved profit and freedom.

My own business school also explored an area where demand exceeded supply. The faculty discussed setting ourselves apart by focusing on teaching and promoting social entrepreneurship. Social entrepreneurship is using business solutions to solve societal problems.

One form of social entrepreneurship is issuing micro-credit. Micro-credit involves granting tiny loans across the world to the poorest of the poor, such as beggars. Amazingly, these individuals have turned their whole lives around with these pittances, sums as low as $20. Incredibly, over 95% of the borrowers pay back the loan in full with interest.

For example, a bank or organization might give a loan to a poor family, who owned one chicken, so they could now get two chickens. It seems like no big deal, except before the bank loan, to avoid starving to death, the family had to eat the first chicken's eggs and had nothing left to sell. Now, because of the bank loan, they had surplus eggs from the second chicken. They could sell the eggs, make a profit, buy more chickens, sell even more eggs – and over time turn their whole lives around!

Micro-credit and other forms of social entrepreneurship are growing rapidly. Muhammad Yunus started this surge by opening the Grameen Bank in Bangladesh, which granted these tiny loans. In 1997, about eight million people had received these loans; in 2004, almost 100 million. In 2006, Muhammad Yunus won the Nobel Peace Prize for his efforts. Dozens of foundations and thousands of corporations are now starting, or otherwise supporting, social entrepreneurship programs. Today there are well over 4,000 institutions that grant micro credit.

Every day, in my role as an entrepreneurship professor, I get multiple emails about the topic. The thirst for knowledge about starting social entrepreneurship programs is amazing. Although universities across the country are starting to offer seminars, workshops, courses and majors, they are not keeping up. Demand for programs exceeds supply. Arguably, my school might avoid direct competition and thrive by serving this area.

Another area in which demand exceeds supply is organic foods. In recent decades, consumption of organics has increased annually between 15 to 30 percent, compared with 2 to 4 percent for all foods. Demand for organics is outstripping the capacity of the estimated 10,000 organic farms, making finding sources of supply one of the key concerns in the industry. Furthermore, many consumers of organics want their products to be locally grown, which creates even greater shortages.

To address this need, Julie, an entrepreneur I've worked with, started a company that delivered locally grown organic foods to people's homes. Given the scarcity of supply and the unmet demand, Julie was able to increase her revenues seven fold in just one year. Her marketing budget was $0.00. She counted on word of mouth and could hardly keep up with her business's growth.

***Avoiding Traps Relating to Demand Exceeding Supply.*** As with the other tactics, there are mistakes one can make when forming an idea based upon entering a market where demand exceeds supply.

***Avoid rapidly vanishing surplus demand.*** One of the most important mistakes relates to whether the surplus demand will last long enough to profit from it. In part, this depends upon whether the demand is just a fad. I would argue that social entrepreneurship is not a fad. Unfortunately, poverty is going to be with us for a while, and social entrepreneurship is a solution that is self sustaining. For example, in the case of micro-credit, the lenders get their money back and can then give out more loans to others in need.

The other factor that could eliminate surplus demand is the speed and ease in which suppliers can enter the market. Universities competing on the basis of their social entrepreneurship programs might indeed find this problematic. For the most part, in order to compete, the faculty in the colleges just need to gain more knowledge about social entrepreneurship and then disperse that knowledge. Arguably, faculty members excel at these two practices. Hence, suppliers of knowledge about social entrepreneurship might grow rapidly.

In contrast, the demand for organic foods gives every indication that it will continue, and that suppliers may have a tough time keeping up. Growing organic foods is tricky and often takes years to become "certified organic".

***Be able to surmount barriers to entry.*** Unfortunately, entrepreneurs considering entering markets where demand exceeds supply make another mistake. They forget to ask whether they can surmount barriers to entry. Barriers to entry are obstacles that keep companies out of industries and may be the reason why there is surplus demand. Examples of barriers to entry include specialized knowledge, advanced technology, and large amounts of money or other resources.

Heartware Inc. serves as an excellent example of a new venture that never really entered its industry. Heartware's primary product was a medical device that could diagnose heart problems without requiring invasive surgery. Impressively, the device was, by far, more accurate, less risky, and less expensive to use than any other system on the market. In addition, given that healthcare costs were rising at an alarming rate, the demand for cost saving medical equipment far exceeded the supply. It was not surprising that Heartware's founder, Gerry Seery, dreamed of future riches.

But to turn his dreams into reality, he had to overcome many barriers to entering the industry, all of which were exceptionally high for new medical equipment companies. In fact, the very reason why demand for medical equipment exceeded supply was that it was so difficult to enter the industry. So instead of becoming a success story, Seery's company went bankrupt. He had to close his doors less than a year after starting. I will return to this example and discuss the barriers he faced in detail in the next chapter.

## An Analogy: How to Beat Larger, More Experienced Competitors

I'll sum up this chapter with a little story. My wife and I recently went on a canoe trip with another family who had a 4-year-old child. The boy was very alive and full of humor. Our two families often took walks down wooded paths together.

Periodically, with no warning, the 4-year-old would bolt and start running as fast as his little legs could take him. He'd last for maybe 30 seconds, then stop all of a sudden and turn around to

look me directly in the eyes. Then he'd throw his hands up in the air and start jumping up and down declaring with a smile, seemingly twice as big as his face, "I win, I win, I win!!"

Now I had not been aware of the fact that he was racing me. I didn't know quite when the race started. I didn't know what path the race was on, and I didn't know when the race was supposed to end. Needless to say – he won every time.

My advice to you is to be as smart as this tot. Make up your own rules to avoid competition.

Following this chapter's guidelines means you don't have to be perfect. You don't have to execute your strategy better than the competition to succeed, since you are in a different arena. Importantly, you have some slack since the competition will not be right on your tail. You can avoid stress and have time to think, relax, and enjoy life both inside and outside the business. And you can make much more money while doing so.

The next chapter describes what you need to consider about your future venture's industry. In the process, you will learn how to avoid many risks associated with starting the venture, radically increasing the odds of success.

• • •

# CHAPTER SUMMARY

## Major Ideas

The table below summarizes the specific strategies that you need to use to refine your idea so that your company will succeed and grant you freedom.

## Avoiding Competition

| Tactic | Traps to avoid |
|---|---|
| Serve an unfulfilled need. | Make sure you are serving a real need. Be sure you can really fill the need. |
| Have extraordinary skills. | Confirm that your skills really are extraordinary. Explore whether the extraordinary skills are crucial. |
| Enter markets where demand exceeds supply. | Avoid rapidly vanishing surplus demand. Be able to surmount barriers to entry. |

Go to **TheBalancedEntrepreneur.com** for exercises, research and readings related to avoiding competition.

Just click on the tab labeled "Resources".

CHAPTER

# THE INDUSTRY:
## Avoiding Dangerous Traps

• • •

### Outdated Strategy:
Buck industry trends and norms because that is how entrepreneurs often hit it big.

### New "Balanced Entrepreneur" Strategy 5:
Creatively, but rigorously, obey industry rules to minimize your risks and maximize your income.

• • •

It is extremely difficult to overcome industry trends and norms. They have evolved over decades, involve a multitude of participants and contain forces beyond the control of any one firm. While it sometimes appears that very successful entrepreneurs defy industry rules, in reality, they have more often worked within or around constraints in extremely insightful ways. For example, Dave Thomas, the founder of Wendy's, did not try to change the buying habits of the industry's current customers by trying to get families to purchase bigger burgers. Instead, he approached a new market segment.

This chapter identifies three different types of industry constraints that must be recognized up front to avoid your company's untimely end. After identifying each type of constraint, I explain in detail how you can mold your idea so you can operate within that constraint, and not only survive but actually thrive.

## Industry Constraint #1:
## The Most Important Industry Rule

Suppose I told you the answer to one simple question will predict with 80% certainty whether your business idea is likely to make money or whether it will lead to intense struggles, teetering on the brink of collapse, and ultimately complete failure?

Well, the answer to one question will provide that information. What's more, you can find that answer relatively easily. Yet, few other books about starting and planning new ventures even mention the question, much less explain how to find the answer.

So what is this truly miraculous question? Simply this: Is the industry you are thinking of entering attractive? By attractive I mean:

1. Industry sales are growing rather than shrinking.
2. On average, companies in the industry enjoy high profit margins.
3. Firms in the industry have high success rates rather than high failure rates.
4. There is room for a lot of little guys as opposed to just huge competitors.
5. Competitors have a live and let live attitude rather than engaging in fierce battles.

The table on the next page, compiled from **http://money.cnn.com/ magazines/fortune/fortune500/2009/performers/industries/**

**profits/index.html** provides **some** of the information needed to assess whether an industry you are considering entering is attractive. It shows, for fifty industries in 2008, the change in revenue to

## Industry Profitability and Growth

| Industry | Percent Rev. Growth | Industry Rank: Rev. Growth | Return on Revenue | Ind. Rank: Ret. On Rev. |
|---|---|---|---|---|
| Aerospace and Defense | 6.9 | 27 | 7.6 | 13 |
| Automotive Retailing, Services | -11.1 | 46 | -7.9 | 47 |
| Beverages | 4.2 | 33 | 2.9 | 30 |
| Chemicals | 7.5 | 23 | 5.0 | 19 |
| Computers, Office Equipment | 2.2 | 36 | 4.3 | 23 |
| Construction and Farm Machinery | 16.1 | 7 | 5.0 | 19 |
| Diversified Financials | -15.9 | 49 | -0.6 | 43 |
| Electronics, Electrical Equipment | 9.3 | 18 | 6.5 | 17 |
| Energy | 16.4 | 6 | 0.9 | 39 |
| Engineering, Construction | 26.8 | 2 | 2.7 | 31 |
| Entertainment | 3.1 | 35 | -10.0 | 48 |
| Financial Data Services | 11.8 | 14 | 11.7 | 6 |
| Food and Drug Stores | 9.0 | 21 | 1.5 | 35 |
| Food Consumer Products | 9.1 | 20 | 6.7 | 16 |
| Food Production | 15.9 | 9 | 0.6 | 41 |
| Food Services | 9.3 | 18 | 7.1 | 14 |
| General Merchandisers | -2.9 | 41 | 3.2 | 26 |
| Health Care: Insurance and Managed Care | 12.1 | 13 | 2.2 | 33 |
| Health Care: Medical Facilities | 6.9 | 27 | 2.4 | 32 |
| Health Care: Pharmacy and Other Services | 11.6 | 15 | 3.0 | 28 |
| Home Equipment, Furnishings | -9.2 | 45 | 0.7 | 40 |
| Hotels, Casinos, Resorts | -5.2 | 43 | -4.5 | 46 |
| Household and Personal Products | 9.0 | 21 | 8.7 | 11 |
| Industrial Machinery | 13.3 | 10 | 6.9 | 15 |
| Informational Technology Services | 6.7 | 30 | 4.5 | 22 |

indicate growth and the return on sales to indicate profitability. In addition to providing the percentages for both categories, it also presents rankings.

| Industry | Percent Rev. Growth | Industry Rank: Rev. Growth | Return on Revenue | Ind. Rank: Ret. On Rev. |
|---|---|---|---|---|
| Insurance: Life, Health (mutual) | -1.2 | 39 | -3.0 | 45 |
| Insurance: Life, Health (stock) | -7.8 | 44 | 4.6 | 21 |
| Insurance: Property and Casualty (stock) | -12.6 | 48 | 3.3 | 25 |
| Internet Services and Retailing | 11.3 | 16 | 19.4 | 2 |
| Medical Products and Equipment | 9.9 | 17 | 16.3 | 4 |
| Metals | 16.1 | 7 | 3.9 | 24 |
| Mining, Crude-Oil production | 23.9 | 4 | 11.5 | 7 |
| Motor Vehicles and Parts | -4.4 | 42 | -0.7 | 44 |
| Network and Communications Equipment | 13.2 | 11 | 20.4 | 1 |
| Oil and Gas Equipment, Services | 19.8 | 5 | 10.2 | 9 |
| Packaging, Containers | 1.0 | 37 | 3.0 | 28 |
| Petroleum Refining | 25.2 | 3 | 2.1 | 34 |
| Pharmaceuticals | 7.0 | 25 | 19.3 | 3 |
| Pipelines | 27.3 | 1 | 1.5 | 35 |
| Railroads | 12.6 | 12 | 12.6 | 5 |
| Real Estate | -11.1 | 46 | -13.4 | 49 |
| Scientific, Photographic, and Control Equipment | 7.1 | 24 | 9.9 | 10 |
| Securities | 0.9 | 38 | 10.7 | 8 |
| Semiconductors/Electronic Components | -2.2 | 40 | 1.0 | 38 |
| Specialty Retailers | 4.2 | 33 | 3.2 | 26 |
| Telecommunications | 4.8 | 32 | 5.1 | 18 |
| Utilities: Gas and Electric | 7.0 | 25 | 8.7 | 11 |
| Wholesalers: Electronics and Office Equipt. | 6.1 | 31 | -0.3 | 42 |
| Wholesalers: Health Care | 6.8 | 29 | 1.3 | 37 |

So, after examining the industry you plan to enter, you need to reach an unbiased conclusion. Is the industry attractive? If you answer "No", you have just quadrupled your risk of failing. If you answer "Yes", you have a way, way, way better chance of success. Write down the previous sentence in your notes (you're taking them, right???). Have you repeated the word "'way" three times? It deserves that much emphasis!

It is very important to obtain hard objective data about industries rather than relying on your gut instincts. For example, many people might think entrepreneurs trying to start a restaurant are making a big mistake. After all, aren't restaurants on average not profitable, and isn't the industry shrinking? Nope. Actually the chart above, under food services, shows restaurants are not too far from the middle of the pack with 9.3% sales growth and a 7.1% return on sales.

But, of course, there are five factors associated with industry attractiveness – not just two. So what about the fact that over 90% of restaurants fail in year one – a statistic bandied about on the TV show "The Restaurant"? Well, don't believe everything you hear. The real proportion of failures is about 25% within one year and 60% within three. This is higher than most industries, but still not nearly as bad as most think. At least now you can start making a concrete assessment with real facts.

One of the industries that entrepreneurs enter most frequently that is very unattractive is the hotel industry. It has negative profits and negative growth. There are other statistics one would want to check before reaching a firm conclusion, but it appears that the only thing high in this industry is the percentage of entrepreneurs who go bankrupt. And before they end up broke, they work incredibly long hours and are constantly putting out fires.

## Options if your Idea Falls in an Unfavorable Industry

So what do you do if your industry is not favorable?

*Pick another idea.* Your most straightforward option is to pick another idea for your venture, one which lets you enter a favorable industry. But, before abandoning your idea, you must ask yourself some questions. Were you just exploring the idea out of mild curiosity, or were you in love with it? Are you the type of person who generates new venture ideas so rapidly that you will never be able to pursue them all? Finally, just how unattractive was the industry? If you were just casually checking the idea out, and you have ten other ideas already lined up and it was truly an awful industry – drop the idea – now. Don't try to buck general negative industry trends when you can avoid it.

But, what if your current idea is the only one you have? Or, what if the idea lets you pursue work you love and is your passion? This book is about how to enjoy every day, so following your heart's desire is paramount. Don't give up on your dream, but instead, be creative when pursuing it. But how?

Let's use the restaurant industry as a hypothetical example. Your heart is set on entering the restaurant industry because there are things about it you LOVE. In fact, it is what you always wanted to do. This is your one and only business idea. But, you don't like the fact that the growth and profits are only about average among industries, and even worse, the failure rate is relatively high. Bottom line, the industry is not attractive enough for you.

**In a situation like this you can employ one of the three approaches below.**

*Approach #1: Transplant your current idea into another industry.*
The first step you can take is to probe deeper by asking yourself why

starting a restaurant is your life's dream. What about it makes you think you will enjoy it so much? Then next, investigate whether you can pursue the essence of what you enjoy in another industry.

Perhaps you think starting a restaurant will be fantastic because your greatest joy in life is inventing new recipes – and better yet, you're truly extraordinary at it. You have had training at the most elite culinary school and won international cooking awards – trouncing many of the best chefs in the world.

Now you are ready to ask yourself, "Can I just tweak my idea, keeping what I love about it, so I can build my business in another industry?" Where else could you use your ability to develop great new recipes? You could launch a community based website focused on innovative cooking, write a cook book, start a cooking show, become a consultant for established restaurants, or possibly run a catering business. While some of these industries might be unfavorable, others might be quite promising. If none of these possibilities were ideal, I'm sure we could come up with many, many more. It's well worth spending an extra couple of days trying to figure out how to transplant your dream idea to other industries than to spend years struggling to make a buck working long hours.

*Approach #2: Ride a positive trend.* There are two other strategies that allow you to succeed even if it looks like your idea is in an unattractive industry. These strategies don't even require you to transplant the idea. Remember the little restaurant we talked about in an earlier chapter? Wendy's. Its founder, Dave Thomas, started when the fast food restaurant industry was very mature, dominated by huge competitors, and unprofitable for most participants. Yet, in a few short years, Wendy's became the 3rd largest player, falling right behind McDonald's and Burger King.

How? When an industry is unattractive, you first need to recognize that fact. But, perhaps you can then latch onto a powerful trend outside of the industry that is so strong, it overwhelms the industry influence. Wendy's counted on attracting the baby boomers to its restaurant. The rise of the baby boomers caused an explosion of people in their twenties and thirties. Plus, the boomers often had large incomes, and were being overlooked by the current competitors. By convincing baby boomers to frequent fast food places, Wendy's grew the entire industry and created a source of profits and growth that never existed before. It didn't ignore industry factors – by tapping into a new market, it expanded the industry. I have no doubt that you can refine your idea in several ways so that it taps into a powerful trend.

*Approach #3: Find a favorable pocket.* There is yet another way to compete without directly battling negative characteristics that may make an industry unattractive. Even if an industry, taken as a whole, is going through problems, there are often existing "pockets" within the industry that might be quite promising. A pocket refers to one specific type of competitor or customer.

Fast service casual restaurants are one type of competitor within the restaurant industry. These sit down restaurants successfully combine the quality of informal family restaurants, while matching, or almost matching, the convenience and speed of fast food. If the average growth of the overall restaurant industry does not satisfy you, you might want to consider starting one these. Consumer spending at fast service casual restaurants is growing at almost 20% per year and experts have concluded that current establishments can't adequately meet the demand. And if 20% per year growth isn't good enough for you – combine fast service casual restaurants with certain types of ethnic cuisine to identify areas with truly explosive growth.

Find those favorable pockets, reach into them and pull out the cash. In the next chapter, I explain in detail how you can turn this concept into an art form.

## Industry Constraint #2: Entering the Industry

In addition to exploring the overall attractiveness of an industry, you must examine the barriers to enter the industry. While these barriers protect the profits of established competitors, they cause newcomers countless problems, possibly leading to their failure to close even one sale. In some ways, the biggest and possibly most frustrating danger entrepreneurs face is failing before they have even really started.

Some industries have low barriers, that is, they are easier to enter than others. In contrast, some industries are very difficult to enter, such as the health care equipment industry, mentioned briefly in the previous chapter. In fact, the barriers in this industry destroyed the medical apparatus company Heartware before it even really had a chance. Below I discuss each barrier, and explain the role it played in ruining the fledgling company.

1. *Difficult to access needed technology and know-how.* The more an entrepreneur needs to know to enter an industry, the fewer who can successfully do so. Inventing new medical equipment requires a high level of know-how that blocks many potential entrants. Given that Heartware's founder, Seery, based his company on an already developed sophisticated medical device, he had successfully surmounted this ordinarily huge obstacle. In fact, this was one of the biggest reasons why he believed his company would succeed. But as we will see, the medical equipment industry contains several other equally formidable challenges.

2. *Large economies of scales.* Economies of scales are the decrease in cost per unit that occurs with increased production, because of operational efficiencies. Imagine, for example, the costs of making one car from scratch, rather than a large quantity. You would have to pay retail for parts and could not afford to use assembly lines to decrease production time and expense. That one car would cost a fortune.

   Entrepreneurs who want to enter industries with large economies of scale have to start off bigger to be cost competitive. Seery encountered this obstacle as he realized that the only way he could sell his device at a reasonable price was to mass produce it. He had to spread the cost of his manufacturing machinery over many units. The industry had higher economies of scale than he anticipated.

3. *Strong product loyalty.* Industries where existing companies have clearly distinguished their product offerings from each other often are more difficult to enter. Current buyers tend to be loyal to the companies they already purchased from because their products have unique features. Seery was surprised how loyal doctors were to their current diagnostic equipment – each of which had its own unique characteristics. The doctors and staff would have had to invest significant time to learn any type of new equipment. By the time Seery realized that existing loyalties would be a huge hurdle, it was too late.

4. *Hard to access distribution channels.* With surprising frequency, entrepreneurs fail because they can't access distribution channels, even though people like their products. For example, it is notoriously hard to get supermarkets to carry novel, new foods. Seery misjudged the difficulty of accessing

distribution channels in the medical equipment industry. The industry was governed by strong allegiances between suppliers and hospitals that take years to develop. The high risks associated with medical equipment led buyers to view industry newcomers with suspicion.

5. *High capital requirements.* Simply put, this concept refers to the amount of money one needs to spend to get started. The larger the amount of startup capital and costs, the fewer companies that can afford to enter. Like many others in the medical equipment industry, Seery found he needed to invest much more than anticipated to refine his product prototypes.

6. *Many government rules that deter entry.* The more highly regulated an industry, the more difficult it is to enter. Many entrepreneurs may not have the technological expertise or resources to comply with these regulations. Clearly, the medical equipment industry is highly regulated. In fact, Seery took twice as long and spent more than twice as much as he projected trying to obtain FDA approval.

Bottom line – Seery went through his entire savings in less than a year. He failed to sell one device. The final outcome – bankruptcy! Of course, high industry barriers do more than lead to financial trouble. Struggling to even enter the industry will make it impossible to enjoy your work, or have much of a life outside of your business.

Fortunately, while some industries are quite hard to enter, others are much much easier, as shown in the table below. The table compares barriers to entry in the home cleaning industry to the barriers in the automotive manufacturing industry.

## Barriers to Entering Industry

| | Home Cleaning | Auto Manufacturing |
|---|---|---|
| **Difficult to access needed technology and know-how** | **No:** Most of us know how to clean and we require almost no sophisticated equipment (e.g., just a vacuum, mop, etc.) | **Yes:** Few have the knowledge to build a car, and one needs access to very sophisticated technology. |
| **Large economies of scales** | **No:** You can start with just one house in your spare time. | **Yes:** You must spread the massive cost of your assembly line, research & development, etc. over a huge number of cars. |
| **Strong product loyalty** | **Possibly:** Buyers may or may not feel strong loyalty to their existing maid. | **Possibly:** Buyers may or may not feel strong loyalty to their current car company. |
| **Hard to access distribution channels** | **No:** It is quite easy to reach home owners in order to get them to purchase your service. | **Yes:** It takes an elaborate system of dealerships to distribute your product. |
| **High capital requirements** | **No:** Buy a few cleaning supplies and you are all set. | **Yes:** This one is so obvious; it probably does not require any elaboration. |
| **Many government rules that deter entry** | **No:** This whole industry flies largely under the government radar. | **Yes:** There are multiple safety standards, ecological rules, and employee regulations that companies must meet. |
| **Summary** | Very **easy** to enter. | Very **hard** to enter. |

## Options if your Idea Falls in an Industry that is Hard to Enter

The table above makes it clear that it is much easier to enter the home cleaning industry than the auto manufacturing industry. But what should you do with information like this? Should you trash your initial idea if it is in an industry that is difficult to enter? Should everybody become a maid? Of course not. As my wife knows all too well, my ideal business does not involve cleaning a house!

If your idea involves entering an industry with high barriers, you have many options. Three of the alternatives to cope with high barriers are almost identical to those related to coping with an unattractive industry. First, if you are not overly excited about your initial idea, choose another in an industry which is easier to enter. Second, isolate the essence of your idea and ask if it can be transplanted to a different industry that is easier to enter. Finally, look within the industry to see if there is a group of homogeneous customers that you can access more easily.

In addition to these options, there are two others that are especially effective for hurdling industry barriers.

*Option #1: Eliminating activities.* Firms are involved in multiple activities, possibly including research and development, operations, marketing and service. Often, eliminating certain activities can radically lower barriers to entry. It might, for example, be very easy to provide marketing in the industry but very difficult to provide the actual good or service. Thus, the question becomes: Can you keep the essence of your idea but eliminate those activities which make the industry difficult to enter? If so, you can eliminate one of the biggest dangers posed by many industries.

Julie, the founder of the organic food delivery business discussed earlier, did a masterful job of eliminating activities which would have imposed higher barriers to entry. Typically, organic food is sold at retail stores. But by focusing only on delivery, Julie had almost no space requirements, and needed very little inventory, cash on hand, or equipment. You get the idea – she needed almost nothing to start. The chart that follows compares the barriers associated with opening an organic food store versus those associated with delivering organic food.

The chart makes it clear that the barriers associated with opening a retail organic food store dwarfed those associated with starting an organic food delivery business. The barriers linked to starting the delivery business were practically non-existent. Julie began part-time, with a few friends as customers, some contacts among organic farmers, and the family car. Her total investment – $600, mainly for coolers.

Eliminating activities does more than just lower barriers to entry. It can make your life more enjoyable in three different ways. First, your simplified business can only include those activities that give you the most pleasure – thereby ensuring you will like showing up to work. Second, reducing what you do can eradicate the number one complaint of entrepreneurs – that they are a jack of all trades who is constantly deluged by, and reacting to, a wide variety of emergencies. Instead, simplifying the business will allow you to focus your limited resources on doing one thing very well and achieving a sense of mastery that generates contentment. Last, simplifying the business, and only doing what you enjoy, will leave you with more free time to have a life outside the business and with the energy to passionately pursue the pleasures that life can generate.

## Starting a Delivery Business

| | Store | Delivery Business |
|---|---|---|
| **Difficult to access needed technology and know-how** | **Somewhat:** Running a store is fairly complex, involving many activities including identifying suppliers, hiring people, site location, and merchandising. | **No:** Primarily just need to identify suppliers. |
| **Large economies of scales** | **Yes:** You must have a significant variety of foods and traffic to make sure you can pay for your space and utilities. | **No:** You can start as large or small as you want. |
| **Strong product loyalty** | **Possibly:** Buyers may be loyal to well established companies, like Whole Foods. | **No:** It is unlikely your potential customers are currently receiving a similar delivery service. |
| **Hard to access distribution channels** | **Probably not:** Not very difficult, although you do need to find a good location. | **No:** Your distribution system is a car. |
| **High capital requirements** | **Somewhat:** Space is likely to be expensive and you need to purchase inventory and some specialized equipment. | **No:** Practically none. |
| **Many government rules that deter entry** | **Yes:** Selling food products out of a retail establishment is highly regulated. | **No:** Farms selling direct to consumers face little or no regulation. By defining the business as purely delivering foods from farms, it escaped regulation. |

It amazes me that so few entrepreneurship books emphasize the importance of deriving business ideas that are simple and relate to what the entrepreneur likes to do. In contrast, this book will return to this theme time and time again, in the chapters that follow.

*Option #2: Partnering.* Another way to enter difficult industries is through partnering. The key is to look for potential partners that have the skills needed to hurdle over the barriers. To his credit, Seery did realize that he needed partners who would give him the credibility he needed to sell to hospitals. However, he realized it way too late and was desperate by the time he started his search for a partner.

## Industry Constraint #3: Basic Industry Requirements

Another critical issue that determines whether or not your business will endure is whether it possesses the basic industry requirements. Basic industry requirements are the different sets of skills, knowledge, and assets that a business needs to survive in a given industry. Having these specific resources doesn't mean the company will do well, but without them, your company is going to encounter severe, probably fatal, difficulties. The dangers of the industry might be insurmountable.

Let me illustrate the concept using my wilderness canoe trip business. The trips were for teenagers ranging from 14 to 18. They were one month long and took place in a remote part of Canada. To have even a chance to succeed in this industry, several things were necessary.

One, you needed to know a really nice area for the trip. I already had the perfect place all scoped out. I had been there many times.

Two, you needed impressive wilderness skills. Cumulatively, I spent years going on trips and receiving extensive outdoor training. I worked on dozens of canoe trips when I was young, rode my bicycle across the country, and winter camped in temperatures dropping below negative 45 degrees – often having to build and sleep in igloo-like structures. I also attended some of the most intensive outdoor leader training programs, including Outward Bound and the National Outdoor Leadership School. Clearly, I had the required wilderness skills.

Three, you needed to have certain safety training. Parents had to know that I could take care of their child if something happened. Problem! I had no official training! Nada!

The last basic industry requirement related to my ability to supervise the campers. No parents were going to send their child with me unless they trusted me to supervise their child. I'll never forget the first sale I attempted to make. I went to the parents' house to give a slide show about the trip. The parents kept asking questions such as, "Do you have any references from parents of former campers?" Nope, it would be my first year running the trips. Mentioning that I helped out on someone else's trips when I was close to the age of their child did not reassure them. "What was your last job?" they asked. The parents were very unimpressed that I had built a very successful company selling energy saving shower heads. It seemed like they wanted to trust me, and gave me multiple opportunities to provide them with reassuring information. "Did you ever work in a secondary school?" they inquired. "No," I responded. Strike one. "What organizations that focus on children, like the scouts, have you volunteered for?" "None," I replied, and strike two. How many children did I have? "Zero," I explained, as I mentally debated whether mentioning how great I was with my dog would mollify their concerns. Strike three – I was out ... of their house.

So how did I survive if I was missing not one, but two, basic industry requirements? I actually had many options, including some that were similar to those discussed earlier in the chapter. I could:

1. Change my idea.
2. Transplant the idea into a new industry which did not have the same requirements.
3. Identify a subgroup within the industry which did not have the typical requirements.
4. Eliminate the need for certain basic industry requirements by getting rid of certain company activities.
5. Partner with an individual or company who had the basic industry requirements I needed.

In addition to these five options, I had a sixth alternative. I could meet a requirement by enhancing my abilities, knowledge and/or background. This was the route I chose in order to meet the "safety training" requirement. As mentioned, I started with no official training. I therefore spent four months attending seminars, classes and a two week long retreat to increase my safety credentials. By the end of the period, I had earned seven different types of certifications including becoming a water safety instructor, a CPR instructor, and an advanced first aid instructor. No parent doubted my safety skills after that.

The other requirement I was missing was a track record showing I could supervise children responsibly. The good news was that it only took me one presentation to realize I somehow had to acquire this critical prerequisite. The bad news was that it was a hard requirement to meet. No amount of training would give me years of experience in a short time. So what could I do?

The answer: I partnered with someone. More specifically, I started working with a well known school teacher. He didn't know of a great wilderness area, lacked safety certifications, and had limited wilderness experience. But he was the living embodiment of trustworthiness.

He was 38 years old and had three daughters, aged 13, 15, and 17. He had spent his entire career teaching in the local junior high and high school. He lived in the same town as my clients his whole life and EVERYBODY knew him. After we began presenting the trip together, over 90% of the parents signed up their child.

I ended up with a very successful company, and I am using the word "successful" in every sense of the term. The business grew steadily and generated a great profit margin. After my first disastrous selling attempt, the company was never in any financial danger – it was virtually risk free and practically ran itself. The only fires I had to put out were those we used on the trip for cooking. As importantly, I had a blast conducting every aspect of the business, be it presenting slide shows or cooking over an open fire. Of course, having five months off a year didn't hurt either. And yes, my income from the trips supported me during those five months.

But I didn't accomplish all this by ignoring the rules. Instead, I realized what the industry rules were and rapidly realized that I had to overcome vital weaknesses.

I rapidly obtained the basic industry requirements I was missing by forming a partnership and obtaining safety training.

Hopefully, from this chapter, you will take away two lessons that are repeated throughout the book. First, your business idea must conform to certain constraints. If it does not, you will likely struggle financially, not enjoy your work, have little free time, and/or have to cope with enormous risks.

That brings me to the second and possibly more important lesson. If you love an idea, don't just abandon it if it does not meet certain criteria. Use the tools in this book to shape your idea at the outset. This will avoid problems and hassles and let you pursue your dream business. Did initially missing basic industry requirements mean that I abandoned my idea to start a wilderness canoe business? No! Did it mean I failed? No! It meant that I recognized potential problems and took the necessary steps to correct them before they hurt my business and made my life miserable. Instead, I started a business and enjoyed a lifestyle I loved.

The next chapter discusses the market and marketing. It contains several simple rules that show how doing less can produce more. You will learn to radically simplify your business life and actually increase your returns. Finally, it will teach you how to employ one simple tactic that can almost GUARANTEE that your idea will be successful.

• • •

# CHAPTER SUMMARY

## Major Ideas

1. It is very important to choose attractive industries.
2. Examine the barriers to entry in your industry to see if you can overcome them.
3. Examine the basic industry requirements to determine if you meet them.
4. The table below provides options if your idea falls in an industry that is unattractive, has high barriers to entry or contains requirements you cannot meet.

## Chapter Five Summary

| Options | Dilemma | | |
|---|---|---|---|
| | Industry is unattractive | Industry has high barriers to entry | Industry contains unmet requirements |
| Pursue a new idea in a different industry | X | X | X |
| Transplant your current idea to a new industry | X | X | X |

| Options | Dilemma | | |
|---|---|---|---|
| | Industry is unattractive | Industry has high barriers to entry | Industry contains unmet requirements |
| Incorporate a positive trend into your idea | X | | |
| Find a pocket within the industry | X | X | X |
| Eliminate activities | | X | X |
| Form a partnership | | X | X |
| Develop relevant skills, knowledge or background | | X | X |

• • •

Go to **TheBalancedEntrepreneur.com**
for exercises, research and readings
related to analyzing industries.

Just click on the tab labeled "Resources".

CHAPTER

# MARKETING:
## Employing Techniques To Increase My Free Time And Decrease My Costs

• • •

**Outdated Strategy:**
Try to get as many customers as possible.

**New "Balanced Entrepreneur" Strategy 6:**
Focus on getting the right group of precisely defined customers.

• • •

More often than not, entrepreneurs put way too much emphasis on maximizing their number of customers at all costs. In their desperation to succeed, they try to cater to everybody's needs. But this makes no sense. None.

First, believe it or not, trying to get every possible customer makes it more difficult to get any customers. You will end up with a fuzzy, unclear message that appeals to no one. People are far more likely to become customers if approached with a targeted message meeting their exact needs.

Second, trying to serve numerous diverse needs will drive you crazy and force you to work incredibly long hours. Each day you will be pulled in a million different directions. Instead, focusing on a precisely defined group of customers with similar needs will radically simplify your business and free up your time to have a life.

Finally, trying to serve diverse desires means you will require a more varied set of resources. This means you will need more financing. Serving fewer needs will radically decrease the amount of money you must raise and put at risk.

This chapter talks about three aspects of focusing on the right group of customers. First, it discusses how initially to choose a great customer cluster. Next, the chapter describes the single best way to almost guarantee that your choice was correct. Finally, it exposes a major error that entrepreneurs make in their quest to increase their customer numbers – a mistake that will definitely make life miserable and increase financing needs.

## Aspect #1: Target a Narrow Group of Customers

The advice above may seem counterintuitive, almost the opposite of what you would expect. In essence, it stresses that less can be more. But, before outlining the reasoning underlying the advice, let me tell you about my nephew's and niece's former business.

Entrepreneurship is in my family's blood. My mom, dad, and both brothers are entrepreneurs. In fact, when my nephew and niece were just ten and eight respectively, they decided to merge their two companies into one. They marketed their merged business using the poster on the next page. Having combined their vast empires, the poster indicated "Alex Co – has everything, does everything." And of course, what's the use of having and doing everything,

# ALEX CO
## Has Everything, Does Everything!

**NEWS:**

**ALEX CO MERGES WITH KATIE KO:** Alex Co and Katie Ko, the company owned by Alex's sister, have merged.

**BOSSES:**
**Alex Simon**
**Katie Simon**

**EMPLOYEES:**
**Max C. Nussenbaum**
**Willie Levitt**
**Kate Nussenbaum**
**Ben Simon**

## CONTACT ALEX CO AND KATIE KO:
**E-mail:**
**ALEX: simoncabot@mediaone.net**
**MAX: maxmuss@rcn.com**

Email us for a FREE catalogue, or to order an item. If you are ordering an item, please give us your address. Send us half the money. When we get that, we will ship your product. As soon as your product arrives, send us the other half. If you would like to pay us in some other way, such as giving the money to us personally, negotiate with us through email. Thank you.

without the policy of allowing customers to negotiate their own form of payment?

Now, almost a decade later, the two are pretty embarrassed about their former business. With age, they have become skeptical about their ability to have and do everything. I am quick to tell them that they shouldn't feel too bad. Many other entrepreneurs make the same mistake. And those entrepreneurs don't have the excuse of being eight and ten.

I'm going to recommend the exact opposite of Alex Co's strategy. To truly make a lot of money, go after a "smaller" market. This will also let you enjoy each workday more, have time for a fulfilling life outside of your job and require less financing.

Importantly though, smaller doesn't necessarily refer to number of people; it refers to the number of different kinds of people. Attack a very well defined market segment. You need to target one select promising group much more intensely than anyone else does.

Are you still skeptical and thinking, "This doesn't make sense to me, Mark. How can going after fewer groups lead to a higher return venture?" Consider the following examples.

The martial arts studio we discussed earlier focused on one type of customer – kids. Starting with almost nothing, it became one of the most successful studios in the state and in the franchise chain.

Wendy's provides an even more impressive example. When Wendy's first started, they didn't care about families, the single largest market segment at the time. Instead, they uniquely focused on just baby boomers. They wanted those young adults. Despite their focused start, they became the 3rd largest fast food chain in less than a decade. They had far, far more sales and profits than other fast food chains except for McDonald's and Burger King.

In case you have higher aspirations than being third in a huge industry, consider this next company. They became number one in the industry despite starting with a narrow approach. At Dell's inception, a time when almost nobody in the mass market knew much about computers, the company focused on computer experts. They targeted information technology executives who purchased computers in volume for their companies. Many of these information technology executives were so knowledgeable that they built their own computers from kits as a hobby.

Enterprise Rent-A-Car is another company that grew to dominate its industry even though it focused on just one market segment. The owners molded every aspect of the company to capture the temporary replacement car market, that is, people who need a rental because their cars were in the shop. In contrast, the main players in the industry were going after everyone including vacation travelers, business travelers, and just as an aside, the replacement market. The end result – Enterprise grew larger than every single competitor, becoming number one in the industry.

***Focusing Increases Profits, Boosts Enjoyment, and Decreases Startup Costs.*** There are many reasons why initially focusing on one well-defined homogeneous group will lead to greater financial success. First, a company that focuses is likely to get a better return on every dollar invested. Let me explain. Assume it costs a new venture $100 to make contact with a consumer to try to convince him to buy its product. The firm only has a $10,000 marketing budget. This means they can only contact 100 potential customers. Here are the entrepreneur's two alternatives:

1. Identify 100 people who have different needs and approach them with a sales message that attempts to accommodate all their needs, or

2. Identify 100 people who have identical needs and tailor your approach and product to those exact needs.

Clearly, the second approach has a greater chance of being effective. With a targeted message and product, people are more likely to buy. You'll get a far better payback on your limited investment.

Furthermore, targeting a particular segment will lead to greater profits because it overcomes one of a new venture's primary obstacles, namely, that it lacks legitimacy. Customers wonder, "Why should I believe that your company can meet my needs if you have no track record?" The following scenario illustrates how targeting addresses this issue.

Let us assume that you have self-esteem issues, possibly, you believe, because you were raised by an alcoholic mother in a single parent home. You decide it is time to improve your self-esteem and locate several companies that offer programs to help. One company, however, explains that it specializes in raising the self esteem of those who were raised by alcoholic mothers in single parent homes. The rest of the companies just discuss general self-esteem issues. So which company do you think you might go to first? Granted this example is a bit extreme, but you get the point. By focusing, you gain automatic legitimacy; it convinces customers you are an expert.

Focusing also is likely to generate more income because it helps new companies overcome the advantages of established firms. Established firms tend to go after many different groups of customers at once. This means they often approach each customer group with a fuzzy message that is not tailored to their exact needs. By specializing, the new venture can break through and provide exactly what the consumer wants.

In addition to providing greater wealth, initially targeting one segment will lead to a more enjoyable life. First, simply put – it makes life much easier. To effectively meet the needs of five distinct groups, you might have to develop five different marketing campaigns, five different customer support systems, and five different types of product. You'll feel pulled in five different directions based upon divergent customer needs.

Conversely, you can try to effectively meet the needs of five distinct groups, with one marketing campaign, one customer support system, and one type of product. But clearly, that challenge is no walk in the park. Why put yourself through that if you only have the resources to approach one group anyway?

The final reason why focusing on one segment makes so much sense is that it will decrease your startup costs. You will not need the money to develop the five different marketing campaigns, five different customer support systems, and five different types of product, as mentioned earlier. It's amazing how much more enjoyable life is when your house is not at risk because it's collateral for a bank loan!

***Determining Your Focus.*** Okay, hopefully you finally accept that you will be better off focusing on a very few segments, probably just one. But there are so many different ways to define your focus, including customer age, geographic area, education, gender, socio-economic class, and occupation. The list is endless and limited only by your creativity. So how do you decide who to target?

Fortunately, there are certain criteria you can use to make sure that your segment is likely to lead you to be very successful. But before explaining the criteria, let me first ask you to evaluate an idea. As you know, in addition to running my business ventures, I have also been teaching entrepreneurship for decades. So, I'm always thinking about how universities can compete. My question is, "What do you think of the idea of starting a university business school exclusively for people with red hair?"

Rate the idea on a scale of one to ten. Assume a ten is, "That's a great idea. I wish I had thought of it. Can I invest in that university?" And a one is, "That idea is really stupid." Do you have the number in mind yet?

What number did you assign? Was it a one or two? Maybe a few wise guys might have rated it a negative ten. I agree that the idea deserves a very low rating – but why? There are millions of redheads in the country. Organizations can clearly identify them and other business schools are ignoring them.

The problem is that redheads do not have any unique needs relating to a business education. This brings us to the first of four important rules you must use to pick a segment.

## Rule #1: The segment has to have a UNIQUE need that your product or service can satisfy.

Take Wendy's. The market they went after, baby boomers, had unique needs that other customers, such as children, didn't have. Wendy's adult customers wanted a better quality product. They wanted a burger that was fresh, hot, juicy and larger.

In contrast, kids were McDonald's and Burger King's primary markets when Wendy's first started. Kids didn't care about quality food. They cared about fun, happy meals, toys, and entertaining spokespeople like Ronald McDonald and the magical, mystical Burger King.

Wendy's also catered to the unique needs of their market in another way. The baby boomers were always in a rush. They needed more than reasonably fast service, and instead wanted to get their food lighting quick. Wendy's response: they became the first chain to successfully implement the drive-through windows.

In contrast, kids often had more time to eat. McDonald's even built playgrounds on site so their customers would stick around and play on the slides. Plus, it would probably be a parent's worst nightmare to order from a drive-through window and then hand their 4-year-old a large, hot burger, just dripping with juice. Ultimately, you know where that burger would end up – on the car seat or the child's lap.

Wendy's young adults demanded a more upscale décor when they ate in the restaurant. So, to take it up a notch, the chain decorated with carpets, Tiffany-styled lamps, and bent wood chairs. This appealed to adults, but certainly not to children. Whether it was food, service or décor, Wendy's tailored everything to the unique needs of their customers – young childless adults.

Dell is another company which took advantage of distinctive characteristics of the market segment they initially focused on, namely, computer experts. At a time when most potential customers were very unfamiliar with computers, and in fact almost afraid of them, computer experts needed far less hand holding. This allowed Dell to sell direct, eliminating the middle man, which in this case was the retail store. By doing so, they purged huge costs from the distribution system. Dell was able to sell their products for a lower price and have higher profits, but only because of the unique characteristics of their clients, namely familiarity with computers.

The company also made their computers to order – a trait their sophisticated customer greatly valued. The experts knew the exact components they wanted. In contrast, at that time, your typical customer found computers so novel and scary, they would probably run away if someone started asking them to specify the RAM,

ROM, pixels and megahertz. Thus, Dell satisfied a unique need of their segment, the desire to order a system to their specifications.

For another example, Enterprise, as mentioned previously, became the biggest in their industry because the segment they served had distinct needs the company could satisfy. Their market was the replacement car customer, that is, people who had their car in a repair shop. So what did these clients need? A company that would pick them up and give them a ride. In contrast, the car renter on vacation or business would just fly into an airport, walk to the rental agency counter and get his car.

My final example is the martial arts studio I mentioned earlier. It focused on children, many of whom took martial arts because they exhibited behavior problems at home and school. Imagine packing upwards of 30 ill-behaved children in the same room to mock-fight each other. Talk about a potential nightmare. This segment clearly has a unique need. They needed instructors who could build a positive environment that would improve the self control and maturity of their students.

So in summary, the first and most important criteria to determine your focus is that the segment must have a unique need that your company can satisfy. I know we have spent some time on this concept, but it is that important! Remember, don't start a business school for redheads.

**Rule #2: The segment should be large, growing, and wealthy.**
The group you target should not be small, shrinking, or poor. That is a path to battling for survival day in and day out. Instead you need to systematically search out a segment that is large, growing, and has financial means.

Let's review a couple of examples that illustrate this concept. Wendy's focused on young adults. The number of baby boomers who had reached young adult status was huge and would grow in the years to come. Many in this segment were yuppies with no children and they had money to spend.

Dell targeted a huge, growing, and rich segment. Dell's experts often bought computers for entire companies. Not only were there more and more businesses acquiring micro computers each year, they often would buy in huge quantities. What a great market to attack!

## Rule #3: It should be difficult for competitors to meet the needs of that segment.

The third criteria to use in selecting your focus is to make sure that competitors can't easily duplicate your efforts and satisfy the segment's desires.

You need unique capabilities in terms of meeting the target market's needs.

Think of the Enterprise example. Why can't Hertz or Avis just start picking up customers? Even before Enterprise became the biggest rental car company in terms of fleet size, gross sales, or profits, they had far more locations than any of their rivals. In fact, they had more outlets than any two competitors combined. Why? They needed more locations so they would have one near the people they were going to pick up, in order to save time and reduce expenses such as gas. In contrast, the nearest Hertz or Avis might have been at the airport, an hour away. Imagine the cost they would incur to aid stranded motorists. To meet the needs of the replacement car market, first off, Hertz and Avis would have to acquire many new locations – no doubt a drawn out and expensive process.

Arguably, this was not even their main barrier. More importantly, they would need to build from scratch entirely new systems to recruit and train employees. Under their current strategy, hiring was simple. Most new employees needed little in the way of special training or skills, and would end up performing a very narrow task. For example, the typical employee might have only needed to learn to efficiently and very quickly check in or check out cars at an airport location.

In contrast, if these companies started focusing on the replacement car market and picking up customers, they would need staff who could spend long periods interacting with irate customers who just had their vehicle smashed up in an accident. Trust me, few people would want to deal with me on the day somebody hits my car. Thus, like Enterprise, the competition would have to learn to recruit and select "friendlier" employees with a much higher level of people skills.

Also, meeting customers offsite makes it hard to predict who would be at the office at any given time. Many employees would be on the road much of the time. Therefore, the companies would need to develop elaborate methods to cross train their people in different functional areas so they could easily fill in for each other. Enterprise has perfected this system.

Finally, the rental car firms would have to find and recruit a much larger number of employees with management potential. They would need many talented individuals to run their huge number of small offices. Enterprise has spent years and vast amounts of capital to develop relationships with universities so they can hire promising undergraduate college students.

Clearly, Enterprise followed Rule 3. Competitors would find it very difficult to meet the needs of Enterprise's market segment.

**Rule #4: The segment should not be crucial to the competition's success.**

Wendy's clearly followed the rule above, when it came out of nowhere and, a few years later, was number 3 in the fast food restaurant market. Before McDonald's and Burger King realized it, Wendy's became a major player in the industry.

How did this occur? McDonalds and Burger King were very slow to react because Wendy's wasn't stealing customers from them. The two served families and kids. In contrast, Wendy's served those baby boomers that currently weren't eating at fast food establishments.

In summary, focus on one well defined market. This is a great way to decrease your resource needs, which will in turn decrease your financing needs. You'll sleep better at night. This strategy will simplify each and every working day and avoid pulling you in multiple directions. Finally, if you use the four rules I provide to pick your segment, you can actually make far, far, far more money than you dreamed possible.

## Aspect #2: Make the First Sale Early

The first part of this chapter examined criteria for selecting which market segment to approach. But is there a way you can really know if you selected the right segment? Can you avoid making a large investment only to go off in the wrong direction, possibly struggling for months or years trying to recover?

In a word, yes. It is amazing how easy it is to almost guarantee that you focus on the right segment. Are you ready ... here's the key – very, very early on, you need to try to sell your product. I am amazed by the number of entrepreneurs who will sit back and plan and plan and plan, before really testing to see whether their "ideal" market segment really wants their product or service.

**If possible, try making your first sale way before you finish a business plan. The information you gain will at least double the value of your plan.**

Take advantage of the fact that, like never before, you can inexpensively and easily approach potential patrons. Can you, early on, line up a quick temporary partnership with an established player, to see if you can sell your product to their customers? Or try to take advantage of the virtual explosion of new communication vehicles, such as websites, search engines, and specialty publications, all of which will let you reach customers. For example, before you set up an elaborate distribution system or make a major investment, try selling your product on eBay even if it is expensive to produce an initial version. See what price and interest level the auction generates. Email the final purchaser to find out what he liked about the product, why he bought, and what concerns he had. You can also explore whether you can sell the product on a website.

See if you can attract significant traffic to your website using adwords. Adwords is a tool related to Google and has been adopted by virtually every search engine. Advertisers first indicate specific words that they want to trigger their ads, and the maximum amount they are willing to pay each time someone clicks on their ad (known as pay-per-click advertising or ppc). When a person uses Google's search engine, ads for relevant words are shown as "sponsored links" on the right side of the screen or above the main search results.

There is, however, an even better way to try to make early sales. As will be discussed, your best alternative, if at all practical, is to personally contact some potential customers and try to sell them your product yourself.

***Reasons you need to make early sales.*** There are many reasons why trying to make early sales will avoid countless hassles later. The first reason is that attempting to get actual orders is the best way to get reliable information.

To illustrate this concept, I'll convey the results of an exercise I use in the university classes I teach. In class, I hold up my Rolex watch and tell the students the price I paid for it, its features, and how long I've had it. Then they pass it around to examine it more closely. Throughout the process, I answer any questions they have about the watch.

I then ask them if they would purchase the Rolex for one half of its original price. Usually, roughly a third of the students raise their hands indicating that they would. That's pretty good, 33% of the market.

So students have examined the product and have the facts. I have "surveyed" them to determine whether they would buy. Many have indicated they would.

Then something strange happens. I approach individual students who raised their hands and demand the money for the watch. They grow confused and ask me what I mean. I explain, "It couldn't be simpler. You just said you would purchase this watch. So, give me the money."

The excuses then start flying: "I already have a watch." "I wasn't *really* planning to buy a watch." "I don't have the money to spare right now." "My wallet is at home." "I need to ask my wife." The justifications for not buying are endless. Despite hundreds of students over the years indicating they *would* buy the watch, it is still sitting right here on my wrist. No one has come through with an actual purchase.

My point is, don't solely rely on hypothetical answers, like those my students give. **The single best way to find out about how the market really feels about your product is to try and really sell it.**

You start the learning process and avoid locking yourself into faulty beliefs that can lead you to years of struggling.

Even if you don't close the sale initially, you will learn what adjustments you need to make. You will gain better information than if you had spent hundreds of hours searching existing databases, analyzing survey results, or conducting focus groups. If one segment won't buy via one method, test another segment or a different method. You can truly make sure you are approaching exactly the right target segment in exactly the right way. It is all about gathering accurate data early in the process to learn with little risk.

In addition to learning, generating early sales provides another major benefit. It produces early positive cash flow which reduces your financing needs. By far, the least expensive source of financing is your own sales. It can work like a charm. Revenue from early sales of my canoe trips provided about 95% of the cash I needed to start the business. To reserve a spot, customers paid half the cost of a trip months before the first paddle touched the water. I then used this money to buy all my equipment. Even if I had needed to discount the price to secure advance payment, it would have been worth it. Giving the customers a discount sure beats getting loans or selling off parts of the business – both of which can lead to big hassles and sleepless nights.

Of course, many entrepreneurs can't finance their whole business through advance orders. Ironically, though, these entrepreneurs may benefit the most from early sales. Banks and funding sources want some proof that a company can actually sell its product. What is the best proof? Product sales. These sales will diminish the time you'll spend knocking on doors to get money. And ask almost any entrepreneur who has been there – time spent begging investors and lenders is time spent not enjoying your life or business!

Perhaps you are thinking, "Wait, this book is supposed to be about shaping my venture idea, yet Mark's telling me to actually start selling a product." Yes, I am. As soon as you can.

*Alternatives to securing early sales.* Of course, sometimes you won't be able to sell your actual final product for a while. In that case, my advice is to still try to take the sale as far as possible, as soon as possible, with actual customers. Attempt any, or even all, of the following.

1. Develop and sell a beta (i.e. prototype) version of the product.
2. Sell a finished module or part of the product.
3. Secure a commitment or letter of intent to purchase the product in the future.
4. Build a webpage through which people can purchase your product, but stop just short of collecting their money. After they enter shipping information, explain the item is on back order.
5. Use pay per click advertising to try to get customers to your product's webpage.
6. Advertise in magazines that target your market segment and see if you can get customers calling or emailing requests for more information.
7. Develop a list of clients who want to keep informed about product developments.
8. Attend a trade show with a prototype. Book future sales calls based on the prototype.

Granted, some of these methods might be inappropriate for your product or service. Also, make sure that what you are doing is both legal and ethical, as certain types of presales may violate the law in different jurisdictions. But bottom line, at least a few of these testing methods will be "spot on". Try different combinations. Be creative. Come as close as you can to making that sale as early as you can.

*You personally need to make the early sales.* Not only do many entrepreneurs delay attempting to sell their products, when they finally decide the company is ready to approach customers, they avoid like the plague being the person to do the selling.

One entrepreneur I talked with a few years ago was the living embodiment of this. He had developed elaborate screen savers for corporate clients. He had the business financial projections completed. He had all the demographics fully planned. He determined exactly how many computers a corporate client would have to have before it would be worth going after them. Yep, he had planned every detail and was sure of success.

His marketing strategy was to utilize members of volunteer organizations as his sales force. Individuals from groups like the Boy Scouts, Girl Scouts, and high school clubs would conduct fundraisers where they sold the screen savers.

Now I can't say for sure whether or not he had a good idea or a bad idea. But, the big problem was that he had no basis for judging the quality of the idea either. After a year of planning, not only had his company failed to talk to a corporation, he decided he wasn't going to be the person who approached the customer. NEVER, NOT ONCE!

Be sure to personally attempt the sale yourself, to make sure you are not getting filtered information. Do not rely on the perceptions of some employee who tried to sell the product or service. Did he fail to make the sale because potential customers were not interested, or because the salesperson missed his appointment and instead went to a local bar for a few beers? Hate to break it to you, but if it was the latter, there is at least a small chance the salesperson might not tell you. Clearly you want the most accurate information.

You also gain credibility when you sell the product yourself. The entrepreneur who wanted to sell screen savers came to me when I was running a volunteer organization and tried to get my organization involved. But when I asked him about the reaction of customers, he had to explain he hadn't approached any of them, but he was sure we could go into any corporate office and "they would just love the product." When I asked him how to get past corporate gatekeepers, he explained that was our job to figure out but assured us, "it wouldn't be hard."

How credible were his statements, never having done any of this himself? Needless to say, not a penny of the hundreds of thousands of dollars my college volunteer organization raised was from selling screen savers.

Pursuing sales early was a major reason why my first year running canoe trips was so successful. I intentionally held off doing a mass printing and mailing of promotional materials until after I tried selling my product on an extremely limited basis, very early in the selling season and my business's history. As mentioned, after my first presentation (and a little more follow up investigation) I learned that I had to find a partner whose name and background would mean something to the parents. Because I started early, I had plenty of time to do just that. By modifying my concept based on the early feedback, I earned greater first year profits than I had thought possible.

Granted, sometimes personally pursuing face to face early sales may not be practical. But when it is possible, without exception, use it as your first option. Furthermore, regardless of which sales option you pursue, you need to stay personally involved. If your company tries selling the product via eBay, you should be the one to observe the bidding and to "interview", via email, the final purchaser. If you are using pay per click advertising, help choose the words that will generate your ads. Get involved in analyzing the results.

Even if your company isn't ready to sell the actual product and is pursuing one of the eight alternatives discussed earlier, you still need to be the major actor. For example, go to the trade show and try to line up future sales calls, try your hand at selling finished components of your products, and/or call on potential customers to secure the letters of intent.

So to recap, entrepreneurs often erroneously believe that success is created by getting the greatest number of customers. In pursuing this belief, they often pursue too many market segments, and as a result do so in an ill-defined and ineffective fashion. Instead, this chapter recommends that you clearly identify the best segment by making sure it meets four criteria and by attempting early sales to those customers. Once you choose the customer group, you must passionately pursue them by meeting their needs.

## Aspect #3: Pricing.

In addition to trying to pursue too many customer groups, the desire to obtain more and more customers leads entrepreneurs to make another major mistake. They do not charge enough for their product or service; often, they are not even close.

I repeat; **don't sell on the basis of a low price**. Remember, you're not going to have a cost advantage over established firms. You're not going to have economies of scale. The cost of getting new customers is much higher than the cost to retain a customer. Being the first to the market is expensive. You need to maintain your profit margin.

In addition to being at a cost disadvantage relative to established firms, there are other reasons to charge a reasonable amount. Let me walk you through two simple scenarios. In scenario one, assume you sell your product for $1,100. It costs you $1,000 to make and 2,000 people will buy it. Your profit will be $100 * 2,000 or $200,000. Alternatively, in scenario two, you price the same product at $2,000 and it costs you $1,000 to make but now only 200 people will buy it. You again make $200,000 (i.e., $1000 * 200 people).

So you are equally successfully either way right? If you are answered yes, you've forgotten chapter two. Success is not only about money (although money is great stuff.). It is also about enjoying your life in and outside of the business. Under scenario one, you need to be perfect. God forbid, your company manufactures some faulty products in a given month – there goes your whole profit margin. And let me remind you that trying to be perfect is no fun. Under scenario two you have a margin for error and still will have a great profit margin. It is also, generally speaking, way, way easier to serve 200 people than ten times that number. Your workday will be less rushed and more enjoyable, and you will have a lot of free time outside of work to savor life.

As importantly, the higher your profit margin, the less you may need external financing. Internally generated profits are always your most trouble-free and least expensive source of funding. You won't need to spend weeks or months at a time begging for money.

With all this said, let me clarify one nuisance about pricing. It may be advisable to charge a relatively low price, if and only if there is some characteristic of your market segment that lets you radically lower your cost structure. This will allow you to price lower, but still have a nice profit margin built in.

Dell, for example, priced their products very competitively, yet had some of the highest profit margins in the industry. How were they able to do this?

The company sold its computers to computer experts who didn't need much hand holding. These knowledgeable individuals didn't need to visit retail stores to purchase. That meant Dell could eliminate all the costs associated with the middle man, such as retail buildings. Yes, Dell competed in part on price, but their market segment had unique characteristics which lowered Dell's cost. Please don't confuse this example with the generic belief that ill-informed entrepreneurs can win price wars with established competitors who have way more experience, deeper pockets, and huge economies of scale.

But how can a new guy manage to charge a decent amount? Simple – follow the advice in this book. Since you have come up with an idea that does not compete head to head with other companies, they are not limiting your price. By tailoring your product or service to a very specific market segment, you are meeting their exact needs. This means they would be willing to pay a fair price. Finally, since the segment is growing and wealthy, they are able to pay. If you're not confident that your product or service provides enough value to warrant a nice margin, you need to further refine your idea.

In the next chapter, I'm going to discuss the organization itself. Perhaps more than in any other chapter, I'll include tactics that will make you enjoy going to work every day. I will provide one strategy that is perhaps more crucial to building the lifestyle you want more than anything else you've learned in this book. After hearing the strategy, it will seem like the most obvious thing in the world. Yet almost no one ever thinks about it.

• • •

## CHAPTER SUMMARY

### Major Ideas

1. Do not necessarily try to maximize your number of customers.
2. Focus on one segment initially.
   a. The segment should have a unique need that you can fill.
   b. The segment should be large, growing, and wealthy.
   c. It should be difficult for competitors to meet the needs of the segment.
   d. The segment should not be crucial to the success of competitors.
3. Try to gather early feedback by trying to sell to your segment very early in the process.
4. There are many ways to generate early sales, including using Google ad words to solicit advance orders from a website, and selling prototypes to select clients.
5. You should be actively involved in the selling process.
6. If you want to be happy and successful, don't charge too little for your product.

• • •

Go to **TheBalancedEntrepreneur.com**
for exercises, research and readings related
to marketing techniques.

Just click on the tab labeled "Resources".

"Launching my idea"

# PART

## 3

# LAUNCHING MY IDEA

• • •

### CHAPTER 7

THE ORGANIZATION:
Shaping My Company To Increase
My Flexibility And Fun

### CHAPTER 8

FINANCING I:
Decreasing My Need For Funding

### CHAPTER 9

FINANCING II:
Raising Money More Easily

### CHAPTER 10

STARTING:
Turning My Idea Into My Company

CHAPTER

# The Organization:
## Shaping My Company To Increase My Flexibility And Fun

• • •

**Outdated Strategy:**
The key to enjoying your business is choosing to produce and sell a product or service you love.

**New "Balanced Entrepreneur" Strategy 7:**
The key to enjoying your business is loving your daily activities at work.

• • •

The belief that the key to enjoying your business is choosing to produce a product or service you love is a huge commonly shared misperception. In fact, many entrepreneurship books actually teach it. I guarantee that if you must make face to face sales calls for your company to succeed, and you hate that, you will be miserable. If you started out loving the product you're selling, you won't by the time you're done.

Instead, the far more important determinant of enjoyment at work is the activities you perform. These activities will also help determine whether you leave work exhausted or have energy to enjoy your free time.

If you asked me which of the chapters in this book was the most important one, I would tell you that you need to read them all. If you continued to press me for an answer, I'd explain more carefully that all the chapters work together; I'd refuse to pick just one. If you then threatened to break my leg unless I pick one, I would tell you that all this information can be life changing for your personal, family, and business life. If finally you told me you were going to hire a hit man to make me talk and make a choice, I would choose this chapter, seven.

This chapter contains two simple but important suggestions. If you follow them you will enjoy showing up to work and have time to enjoy life outside of your company, all while making money.

## The Most Important Issue

What I'm about to share is more important to your happiness than any other strategy, tactic or concept we've discussed. Yet, no books on entrepreneurship or writing a business plan mention this crucial strategy to business ownership fulfillment.

I'd like to introduce the strategy by telling you about an exchange I had with an old friend who was thinking of acquiring a business. He wrote a comprehensive business plan that laid out how he was going to buy a juice delivery route, work it himself for a couple of years, and then expand to several routes overseeing multiple delivery people. Knowing that I was passionate about helping potential entrepreneurs, especially those who were longtime friends, he asked if I would give him feedback on his plan.

At which point I said, "Absolutely not." He looked at me in surprise and offered me money. I told him that money was not the issue, but that I wanted him to do something more before I looked at the plan. I explained that he had not yet investigated the single most important issue regarding the business.

"What issue?" he asked. "Do I need to incorporate more industry information or talk to more suppliers, or survey more customers and potential customers?"

I responded "No" to all these questions, and to the other dozen questions he asked. Finally he demanded to know what crucial issue was neglected.

Have you, the reader, figured out what I wanted him to do before I would even look at the plan? Only a handful of the hundreds of clients and students I've asked, have answered correctly.

I wanted him to actually work every aspect of the route for two days to determine if he would like what he was about to do day in and day out. Think about it – what can be more important than enjoying your daily tasks? Yet, so many entrepreneurs, entrepreneurship students, and even experts who write about and teach venture creation forget about this issue!

So, he started to work the route. But he only lasted **one** day. He told me, "Mark, it was the most miserable day of my life. I couldn't stand hauling crates, the traffic, or the arguments with customers about payment. Don't look at my business plan."

Now there's nothing wrong with a route for some people. You get exercise, you're not stuck in an office, and you get to interact with people all day. But my message is – and I want you to write this down in big bold letters – **only get involved in a business which lets you focus on tasks that you enjoy**. Otherwise don't do it. Life is precious. Time is precious. Your happiness is precious. Remember to do only what you enjoy!

My brother has become very successful flipping large commercial properties. Once a mutual friend of ours said to me, "Mark, you have been so successful in what you do, why don't you get into real estate with your brother? If you do it right, you can make a lot of money." I almost shot him on the spot.

Commercial real estate is great for some, but I'd hate it. It involves three tasks that I detest. The first is negotiating. To me, negotiating is the single least enjoyable way to interact with people. Second is waiting. You can go for months, and much longer, before making a deal. And no matter how long it's been, you must be willing to walk away if a deal isn't great. You can't rush it. I would go crazy. What an awful lifestyle – at least to me. Finally, commercial real estate requires you to build an extensive network of wealthy contacts, yet another task I hate. Don't get me wrong. Networking is a crucial skill in many, many businesses and it can benefit all parties. There is nothing wrong with it. In fact, there are many positive things about networking. I just personally would not want to enter a business that relies on it more than almost any other business.

Alternatively, I wish you could see me now. I am smiling. I am happy. Why? I am working on a book. Contemplating ideas, researching them, and writing about them is my version of heaven. It's what thrills me and makes me want to wake up in the morning.

And that's what you need to decide about yourself. What type of business should you be in? Not what business do other people think you should be building. It doesn't have to be delivering information like I do and it doesn't have to be flipping commercial real estate like my brother does. It's whatever business that lets you spend your time on tasks you really enjoy.

## OVERALL FIT

Making sure you love the activities your business requires you to do is just the first of four ways the business needs to fit you. Only by emphasizing all four of the ways will your business be ideal for you.

The second way that your business should suit you is that its requirements should match your skill set. Focusing on what you're good at will avoid untold frustration and hassles. It's like starting a race from half way to the finish line.

Take me, for example. While it's true that real estate isn't right for me because I hate negotiating, it also isn't right because I'm not a great negotiator. In contrast, look at this business which involves teaching others how to start a successful business they will enjoy. I love teaching in all its forms, but as importantly, I think I'm pretty good at it. I've won eight teaching awards. I'm never more in my element than when standing in front of a classroom or developing lessons. In fact, when I was just eight years old, my uncle nicknamed me the Little Teacher. He saw how much I loved explaining things.

Third, the business's risk/return profile should match your desires. Some businesses are inherently riskier than others. Some have a greater potential for a higher return. The question is: what do you need to keep you happy? What if hundreds of thousands of dollars, or more, hung on closing one sale? Ask yourself, would I find that exciting or just extremely stressful? If your answer is the former, commercial real estate might be just the thing for you. You might not mind the risk. If you would just find the situation extremely stressful, I'd recommend you pick a new area.

The fourth and final fit relates to your passion. Have you chosen a business that you're passionate about? Does it feel like a higher calling? I know I have been passionate about my businesses, which range from instilling confidence in teens on wilderness canoe trips, to teaching potential entrepreneurs not only how to run a financially successful business, but as importantly, how to enjoy the process. I am giving people the tools to fulfillment, and to me nothing is more meaningful than that. Examine all four forms of fit before launching your venture.

## Outsource

So what are your options if you do not enjoy an activity or are not very good at it, yet it may be necessary to your business? One, you could change your idea, but that might not be necessary. Two, far less drastic, you can hire others to do it. But I actually will argue that even this is not necessarily the most desirable option. Instead, I often recommend that you outsource the activity if possible. Get that down in writing, **outsource**. Put it in big letters.

# OUTSOURCE

*Why outsource?* There are many reasons why outsourcing can make every single day of your life as an entrepreneur more enjoyable and profitable. The first reason is that outsourcing is a great way to control costs. As the previous chapter explained, it allows entrepreneurs to substitute variable costs for fixed costs. Along a related line, it minimizes up front expenses. The company you outsource the production to has to purchase all the manufacturing equipment. You don't have to lay out a penny in advance.

Another benefit of outsourcing is that it may actually be less expensive for your firm overall. The firm that you outsource to may pass on some of the cost savings they achieve through specialization and economies of scale to your company. Minimizing and/or controlling all these costs will help you sleep a lot better at night.

The second reason to outsource is that it alleviates the need to be good at everything – ranging from manufacturing to accounting, and from sales to human resources. Instead, you can subcontract to firms whose experience and expertise may surpass that of established competitors to perform those functions.

Your company will be able to emphasize doing a few things that really matter rather than being a jack of all trades and master of none. Consequently, you will experience the pleasure associated with excellence and avoid the frustrations associated with mediocrity. You can focus on what is most important to your business's success.

Alleviating the need to be good at everything minimizes the entrepreneur's single greatest source of irritation. Outsourcing will curtail the number of fires that entrepreneurs have to put out. Talk to any entrepreneurs and I bet they will tell you that one of the most annoying things they contend with is constant unscheduled "crucial" interruptions. They feel as if they're on a treadmill constantly running, only to go home exhausted, having made no progress. If you decrease the number of areas you directly oversee, many of those interruptions magically disappear.

Now, don't get me wrong, you can't completely ignore tasks even if you outsource them. You have to select the right firm and monitor what they do. That, however, is truly a piece of cake compared to hiring the right individual or individuals, training them, monitoring them, rewarding them, and then repeating the entire process again when they leave after a year.

***What to outsource.*** In order to decide what to outsource, you should first decide what not to outsource. Try to keep in-house only those tasks that are most critical to your success. There are many questions you can ask yourself to determine which tasks to keep:

1. What are you really good at?
2. What is the main reason why customers will buy from you or your business?
3. How are you differentiating your product or service?
4. What 20% of tasks generate 80% of the results?

After answering the questions above, try to outsource as many of the other tasks as possible. There are many organizations that can take over operations, accounting, human resource management, and even manufacturing. So decide what is most important to your business and outsource the rest.

You have just read how to narrow your business's activities so that you are primarily doing what you enjoy. One of the side benefits of this includes greatly reducing the amount of financing you need at the start of your venture and throughout its life. The next chapter builds on this one by discussing other methods to reduce the amount of necessary outside capital.

• • •

# CHAPTER SUMMARY

## Major Ideas

Although relatively short, this may be the single most important chapter of the book. Following the simple advice contained in this chapter will literally make each and every day running your venture more enjoyable. The chapter revolves around two very simple rules:

Rule 1: Make sure your idea necessitates focusing on doing daily activities you will enjoy and are good at.

Rule 2: Through outsourcing, eliminate as many of the other activities as you can.

Remarkably, despite the incredible power of these two simple rules, almost no other entrepreneurship book focuses on them!

• • •

Go to **TheBalancedEntrepreneur.com**
for exercises, research and readings related
to shaping your company.

Just click on the tab labeled "Resources".

CHAPTER

# FINANCING I:
## Decreasing My Need For Funding

• • •

**Outdated Strategy:**
Achieving sales projections is the major path to success.

**New "Balanced Entrepreneur" Strategy 8:**
Figuring out how to prosper even if one doesn't initially generate the sales expected is the major path to success.

• • •

You need to develop financial projections. The process increases your understanding of your venture idea, helps you refine faulty ideas, and is critical for raising money.

But a major problem develops when entrepreneurs begin to act as though their projections will accurately reflect reality. This leaves them ill prepared for the financial swings that often occur. Most entrepreneurs don't, and can't, develop accurate financial projections for their first year or two of business because they are journeying into the unknown. In fact, nine out of ten entrepreneurs forecast first year sales that are more than 40% higher than their actual sales, and six out of ten overestimate their sales by more than 60%. While the strategies in this book, such as making your first sale early, will make your forecasts more accurate than most, developing projections that are even close to reality will still be a daunting task.

The good news is that this chapter will teach you steps you can take to assure you have a good life and a great business even if your early sales projections are off. While you can't predict with 100% accuracy how much revenue you will generate, to a startling degree, you can eliminate the consequences of sales falling short. You can, for example, eliminate the need to work extremely long hours, for little or no pay, just to keep your doors open. What's more, even if you sell less than expected, if you follow this chapter's advice, you can still achieve at least modest profits in the short run, and substantial profits soon thereafter.

Are you wondering how the chapter's "Balanced Entrepreneur" strategy relates to the question posed in the chapter's title? How does following a strategy that allows you to prosper, even if you overestimate sales, help decrease the financing you need (the chapter title)? The answer – in the most important way possible.

Let me explain. The strategies that allow you to prosper even if you miss your projections, will reduce your up front costs and cut your overall expenses throughout the business's early years. This reduces the amount of financing you need.

Why is this so important? Let me put on my professor's hat to answer that question. Hunting for money sucks. (Oops, that wasn't stated very "professorially," was it, but it had to be said.) The process represents the antithesis of being a balanced entrepreneur. (Whew, that hopefully sounded more sophisticated; I was worried "they" were probably about to revoke my Ph.D.) Time spent begging for money is not time spent:

1. making your business more profitable.
2. engaging in pleasing business activities.
3. enjoying your family and friends.

Don't be misled, even though the first three letters of fundraising spell "FUN", it's not!

Even if the tactics recommended in this chapter don't totally eliminate your need for outside funds, they will make it far easier to generate the capital you do require. By decreasing the amount you need, you can approach fewer funding sources, ask each source for less, and target only those sources that are easiest to deal with rather than the ones who will make your life a living hell. The tactics also decrease the likelihood of unexpected emergency cash shortfalls. As you might expect, financiers don't want to give money to someone who is desperate.

As you read further, though, you need to keep three ideas in mind. First, remember that while beneficial, tactics that minimize your costs are not a reason why you will succeed in the long run. They are at most a temporary way to lessen all the cost advantages of larger, established firms. Furthermore, they do not generate a sustainable advantage; eventually you will outgrow many of these methods. You need to compete based on one of the ways stressed in chapter four to build a successful and sustainable business.

Second, follow my recommendations early before you really need them. Don't use them to "save" your business. Use them as soon as possible to make sure your business never needs saving. Unlike most of the other tactics in this book which many founders never realize, countless entrepreneurs eventually and independently stumble upon some of the tactics I'm about to share. But, they've waited too long. Often they go bankrupt before the tactics take effect. If they get lucky, the strategies might pull them out of their decline, but they're still looking at years of suffering, staying awake at night with worry, and cutting every luxury, no matter how small, out of their personal life. That assumes, of course, they have time for a personal life.

If only they had implemented the ideas in this chapter sooner, before they really needed them, they would've been able to pay their bills, sleep peacefully, and enjoy a life outside of the business.

Finally, you may note that slightly different assumptions underlie parts of this chapter than underlie the rest of the book. Throughout this book, all my suggested tactics represented win-win scenarios. For example, if you pick the right narrow market segment, you can have more free time outside of work and make more money. Or if you enter an attractive industry, your company is likely to be more profitable and face far fewer risks. In addition, if you outsource the right activities, you will enjoy each workday more and achieve a much higher return on investment.

While much of this chapter allows for the same win-win mentality, a few of the suggestions might entail trade-offs. For example, initially you may choose to run your business out of your house to save money, even though it might be harder to avoid distractions. Alternatively, you may not want to follow my recommendation to share certain assets with another company because, in your mind, the savings are not worth the inconvenience.

Only you can determine which trade-offs are worth it. I have no question that using a room in my house as headquarters for my wilderness canoe trip business was the right move. It involved little or no inconvenience and saved a great deal of money. Alternatively, if I could travel back in time, I would have never chosen to live in my import business's warehouse regardless of the savings. With the techniques I know now, I could have taken enough out of the business to get a decent place. Make sure to consider all the benefits you want to achieve as a balanced entrepreneur, before making your choices.

The remainder of this chapter is divided into two major sections. The first section recommends tactics that will minimize the amount of financing you need to start the venture. Next, the chapter focuses on how to avoid frantically begging for more money after you start your venture.

## Minimizing Your Initial Investment

If you have been reading this book carefully you probably have already learned more about how to minimize your initial investment than you realize. Let's review some of the principles we've already covered that will decrease how much money you need to pursue your venture idea.

1. *Don't directly challenge established competitors.* You can save money by avoiding head to head conflicts with existing companies. Your venture idea should not involve trying to steal their customers and overcome pre-existing loyalties, because this may require large up front costs. Instead, it should develop new markets.

2. *Pursue ideas that let you compete in industries with low barriers to entry.* This will minimize your startup costs. Correspondingly, avoid ideas that force you to contend with high barriers to entry. This is especially true if you need significant capital to enter the industry, or if you have to achieve large economies of scale to compete. Industries that grant large economies of scales put smaller firms at a major disadvantage, thereby forcing entrepreneurs to spend large amounts to start off.

If, however, your heart is set on competing in an industry that ordinarily has high barriers, use some of the methods discussed in chapter 5 to make it less expensive to enter.

3. *Your idea should primarily appeal to one narrowly defined market segment.* Targeting one precisely defined market greatly decreases your need for up front capital. You can compete without paying for a diverse set of resources to meet a diverse set of customer needs. Furthermore, by targeting your campaign toward very specific customers you can maximize the effectiveness of every dollar spent.

4. *Make your first sale early.* Trying to generate sales early in your business's life not only provides insight about your idea's feasibility and which market segment to pursue, it also generates cash. Sometimes early sales to customers can be used to finance your whole business. Plus, you can use these early sales to provide references to other prospects, allowing you to get their money sooner as well.

    My wilderness canoe trip business illustrates the importance of collecting funds early. I got paid in full in January to run summer trips for kids. Before my first trip even started, I received enough money to buy all my equipment – much of which would last for years and possibly even decades. How cool was that?

5. *Outsource.* Outsourcing or narrowing the scope of your activities can greatly reduce the amount of your up front investment. As you may recall, by narrowing the scope of her operations to just delivering organic food, Julie was able to start her business for less than $600. Compare that amount with what she would have needed had she opened a retail store or started her own organic farm.

There are many activities you can outsource. Consider using an answering service or virtual assistant instead of staff. In addition to decreasing labor costs, having fewer employees on site lets you reduce your operating space. Importantly, obtaining space can be associated with large up front expenses.

In addition to the tactics above, here are several new ones you can use to minimize your startup costs.

1. *Plan for your best case scenario, but don't invest in it.* If you are like most entrepreneurs, some of your predictions may be overly optimistic. Don't spend money based on them, especially if those expenditures are largely irreversible. You can usually make adjustments later when the sales start pouring in. Although you shouldn't lay out the cash, do try to make arrangements for the future in case you generate more demand than anticipated. If you hit the numbers, you will be shocked at how much a little advance preparation will let you ramp up.

   Might expanding via a piecemeal approach cost you a little more than if you had purchased everything at once up front? Perhaps. Do I care? In a word, NO. Given the high likelihood of overestimating sales, the amount you might save from one big purchase is rarely worth the risk. If you overinvest, you have at best an intense struggle, and at worst, a complete and total failure from which you never recover. In the unlikely event that you have better than expected sales, you are still in fine shape. Now that you know what your demand really is, you can plan accordingly.

   When I started my canoe trip business, I followed the strategy above. I found a great deal on used canoes, however,

I didn't know how many to get. I decided to be conservative and only get enough to accommodate my most pessimistic predictions. Because the seller was charging so little for the boats, I knew he would sell out soon and I would not be able to get even close to the same price anywhere else. So I offered him a non-refundable $300 dollar deposit that would hold 10 more boats for me for three more months. If I bought the boats the money would go towards them, if not, he kept it. He agreed. My sales exceeded my wildest projections and I got the additional canoes. Sure I put $300 at risk, but are you crying for me?

Planning for your best case scenario, but not investing in it, is such an important tactic that I'll illustrate it with another example. I started a business that sold energy saving products. My main supplier gave incredible price breaks as one's order quantity increased, meaning my per unit cost for products depended upon whether I purchased enough to accommodate my pessimistic, expected or optimistic predictions.

I went with the pessimistic prediction, but I negotiated that I would get a special additional discount if I reordered within three months of my first order. Bottom line, I had enough demand to place a larger order three months later, so saved some money. In truth, though, I could have ordered enough in my first order to accommodate my expected prediction and saved even more money.

It does not bother me that I did not maximize my profit and played it safe. I followed the philosophy that I'd rather be safe than sorry early on in a venture history. I still made an okay margin and was able to enjoy my work and have the time for a life at home. Over the course of the next couple of years I became proficient at ordering the exact right amount. In contrast, if I had ordered enough up front to accommodate my expected prediction and not sold enough, I would have created huge cash flow problems. These problems would have put my business at risk, caused undue stress, and definitely cut into my personal life, making me a slave to selling my product.

2. *Buy what you need, not what will make you feel important.* Too often entrepreneurs make investments to gratify their ego, not to build their business. When you start your business, do you really need your office in a penthouse, a location in a prestigious neighborhood, or top of the line furniture? Sure, part of me would have liked an impressive office when I ran my wilderness business, but I was always meeting clients at their homes, so why bother.

3. *Purchase used equipment or buy direct from manufacturers.* If it doesn't make you a profit, try to save on it. This is exactly what I did when purchasing canoes. Given the power of the Internet, you can find bargains like never before. Search them out.

4. *Operate out of your house.* Is it practical for you to operate out of your house? It was with my canoe trip business, and it saved me a lot of money. Plus, Uncle Sam provides a slew of deductions. Of course, consult with an accountant, but basically to qualify for home office deductions you just need to meet two conditions. First, the space you are claiming must be exclusively devoted to, and regularly used by, your business. It cannot be used for anything else. Second, it must be your principal place of business or a location where you meet with customers in the normal course of conducting business.

So what additional savings are there if you use your home as an office? You can deduct part of your:

- property taxes,
- utilities,
- homeowner's insurance,
- home's depreciation,
- painting, and
- repairs.

And this is all in addition to eliminating the need to buy or lease a separate facility. Not too bad a deal.

5. *Share expensive resources.* Be it a drill press, copy machine, space or some other costly asset, can you find someone with which to share it? If the company next door has a copy machine that is idle 90% of the time, can you reach an agreement with the owner? This single practice might radically decrease the amount it costs you to run your business. One crucial word of advice – structure the deal in such a way that either party has an out if it is not working for them. Put the agreement in writing. Remember it is all about developing a work life you love, not spending hours a day quibbling about whether you use a copier 33% or 40% of the time.

Believe it or not, there may be a growing company out there that will let you use space for free. Perhaps their facility is bigger than they currently need; but why should they let you use it? Well let's use the example of a personal fitness exercise studio with which I worked. The managers had a free office, which they let a separate diet business use. Each week, the exercise studio had dozens and dozens of new people literally walking through their facility to get nutritional counseling to help them lose weight. And what did the people sometimes do? You got it – bought sessions at the exercise facility. The marketing cost of getting the new clients was zero dollars and zero cents. So ask yourself, is there a business that has extra space that your presence will benefit?

6. *Make your product to one customer's specification, and then expand.* This tactic is closely related to the idea of getting the first sale early. More specifically, tailor your idea to meet one customer's precise needs. Assume, for example, your idea is to develop a generic software package that helps manage any personal fitness studio. Instead of starting with a nonspecific package that can meet every customer's desires, start by making one specific package for one specific company. You can then use the knowledge you gained, the code you developed, and the money you earned to produce the generic version of the product that can be mass marketed.

Consulting firms often employ their own version of this rollout method. They will consult with a client in a given industry about a common problem. They can then use the research they conducted and framework they generated to consult with others in the industry encountering similar challenges. So my question to you is: is there a creative way you can adapt this method and save yourself a lot startup costs?

## Making Sure You Don't Run Out Of Cash

Minimizing up front expenses is one thing, but how do you make sure you are not constantly running out of cash throughout your business's life? Trust me, one of the few things that is worse than having to plead for cash to start the business, is to have to plead for cash to keep your doors open after starting, while you are still trying to conduct the business's daily activities.

Before I discuss the specifics of what you can do to make sure you don't have to constantly seek financing, I will share an exercise I do with my class. First, I pass out copies of an income statement to my students. An income statement shows how much profit a company makes, at least on paper, over a period of time. For example, if a company made a huge sale, the income statement would indicate the sales revenues, as well as the corresponding expenses and profits.

After explaining the income statement to the students, I ask what entrepreneurs should do with their income statement. I get a wide range of answers before I show them the "correct" one. I tear up the statement. Yes, right in front of the whole class, I rip the income statement into tiny pieces and throw each and every bit of it in the garbage.

Next, I give each student a copy of a company's balance sheet. A balance sheet is a snapshot of a business's condition at a specific moment in time. It can be used to measure many aspects of a firm's financial health. I then ask the students what entrepreneurs should do with balance sheets. A few proceed to rip it up. I, of course, lavishly praise these students for their insightful answer. After which I mimic their actions.

Finally, I give a cash flow statement to the students. The cash flow statement shows when dollars come in and when they go out. I ask what entrepreneurs should do with the cash flow statement. As the students start to rip up their copies, I yell, "Stop!"

After clearly indicating that their actions are not only wrong but downright sacrilegious, I proceed with the appropriate action. I very gently and with a great deal of respect put the cash flow statement on a chair in front of me and get on my knees. I then bow down and start worshipping it.

Okay, I admit it, **the exercise with my students grossly overstates my point**. Entrepreneurs most definitely need to understand their balance sheets and income statements. And of course, they shouldn't actually tear these documents up and throw them away. With that said, however, I am going to keep doing this exercise because it drives home an all important message.

The message is that **cash flow is the life blood of a new business.** Cash flow is king. Cash flow counts more than anything!

Let's walk through a simple example to show why cash flow is so crucial to entrepreneurs starting new ventures. By definition you start with zero sales. So you must grow your sales to survive. Assume a new venture starts with an initial investment of $4,000 and uses it to generate $5,000 in sales its first quarter. Every dollar of sales generated, in total, costs the company 80 cents. Early in its life, the company increases it sales by 50% every quarter. I know this growth rate seems high, but it actually may not be since new ventures usually start with so few sales it is easy to increase them by a significant percentage. Sounds like the venture is doing just fine, right? After all, look at the table, labeled "Profits", and corresponding graph that follow.

Now for the rub. A difficulty arises because you need to spend cash in the current quarter to generate future sales. For example, you will need to spend now on advertising, inventory and labor to make the products that you will sell next quarter. But current revenues might not cover the costs associated with next quarter's sales, because each quarter, sales are growing at 50%. Let's examine quarter 2, for instance, in the table labeled "Cash on Hand". Your current revenues were $7,500 in quarter 2, but you need $9,000 in quarter 2, to generate quarter 3 sales of $11,250. You are short -$1,500 for that quarter, plus another -$1,000 from the previous

## PROFITS

| Initial Investment: | $4,000 |
|---|---|
| First quarter sales: | $5,000 |
| Costs associated with sales: | 80% |
| Growth in sales: | 50% |

| | Revenue | Cost | Quarter Profit | Cumulative Profit |
|---|---|---|---|---|
| Initial Investment | $ 4,000 | | | |
| Quarter 1 | 5,000 | 4,000 | 1,000 | 1,000 |
| Quarter 2 | 7,500 | 6,000 | 1,500 | 2,500 |
| Quarter 3 | 11,250 | 9,000 | 2,250 | 4,750 |
| Quarter 4 | 16,875 | 13,500 | 3,375 | 8,125 |
| Quarter 5 | 25,313 | 20,250 | 5,063 | 13,188 |
| Quarter 6 | 37,969 | 30,375 | 7,594 | 20,782 |
| Quarter 7 | 56,953 | 45,563 | 11,391 | 32,173 |
| Quarter 8 | 85,430 | 68,344 | 17,086 | 49,259 |
| Quarter 9 | 128,145 | 102,516 | 25,629 | 74,888 |
| Quarter 10 | $ 192,217 | $ 153,773 | $ 38,443 | $ 113,331 |

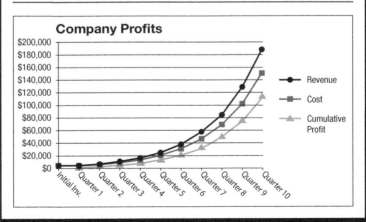

## CASH ON HAND

| | Revenue | Amount Needed | Shortage for Quarter | Cumulative Cash on Hand |
|---|---|---|---|---|
| **Initial Investment** | **$ 4,000** | | | |
| Quarter 1 | 5,000 | 6,000 | (1,000) | (1,000) |
| Quarter 2 | 7,500 | 9,000 | (1,500) | (2,500) |
| Quarter 3 | 11,250 | 13,500 | (2,250) | (4,750) |
| Quarter 4 | 16,875 | 20,250 | (3,375) | (8,125) |
| Quarter 5 | 25,313 | 30,375 | (5,063) | (13,188) |
| Quarter 6 | 37,969 | 45,563 | (7,594) | (20,782) |
| Quarter 7 | 56,953 | 68,344 | (11,391) | (32,173) |
| Quarter 8 | 85,430 | 102,516 | (17,086) | (49,259) |
| Quarter 9 | 128,145 | 153,773 | (25,629) | (74,888) |
| Quarter 10 | 192,217 | 230,660 | (38,443) | (113,331) |
| Quarter 11 | $ 288,325 | | | |

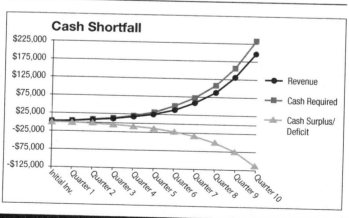

quarter for a total of -$2,500. Bottom line, every single quarter, you are running out of more and more funds. Granted this example is greatly simplified, but it captures a reality.

Worrying whether you can afford your rent in a given month, dodging creditors, and constantly begging for money does not lead to enjoying your life. Furthermore, these energy draining, time consuming activities will divert you from actions that lead to increasing the business's profits.

So a key to both financial success and life success is to figure out, from day one, how you can improve your cash flow. There are two possible avenues. First, make sure your idea naturally generates a positive cash flow. The personal fitness facility I discussed earlier was based on an idea that had nice cash flow ramifications. Its clients paid up front for a service they would primarily use in the future, blocks of one hour workout sessions. The greater the block of sessions, the greater the total amount paid (even though the owner gave a slight discount) and the further in the future the client would receive the service. Many clients purchased enough sessions to last the entire year!

Second, if your idea does not naturally generate surplus cash, you can emphasize any combination of four levers to improve your cash flow. The four levers are:

1. charge more for products or services.
2. spend less.
3. collect revenues sooner.
4. make payments later.

Each of these levers can be implemented through a wide range of actions. You are only limited by your imagination. I've listed some actions below to get your creative juices flowing. Most of this list is brand new, while the rest has been mentioned in another context.

1. *Don't charge too little.* Your initial idea must provide enough of a unique benefit that your customers will pay far more than your cost of delivering your product or service. Since you need to fund tomorrow's growth with today's revenues, make sure you charge every penny that your product or service is worth. If the company discussed in the previous tables and figures had raised its prices by just 20%, it would not have had any cash shortages. Instead of every $1.00 of sales costing the company 80 cents, every $1.20 of sales would have cost 80 cents. This represents a 50% mark up which would have covered the company's 50% growth rate.

   Making sure your price reflects the full value of your product or service also gives you room to offer a discount to get customers to pay early, as discussed next.

2. *Discount prices to collect cash up front.* You need to consider discounting your price for customers who pay in full on or before delivery. My wholesale company offered fantastic savings to stores that paid us up front.

   When deciding how much to discount prepayments, don't just calculate the amount of bank interest you can earn by getting your money earlier. Prepayments generate many other monetary and non-monetary benefits. They eliminate the cost of collecting accounts receivable and the possibility of non-payments, and perhaps more importantly, can diminish the possibility of needing a loan. This, in turn, helps you avoid expenses and time associated with writing and presenting business plans. To quote a television commercial – the value of not having to grovel for money – priceless.

3. *Collect quickly.* If you do offer credit, start collecting immediately after the grace period. Don't wait till the end of the month. Call with a polite reminder sooner rather than later.

4. *Be careful about extending credit.* Even though you might feel anxious about sales, don't extend credit to companies or individuals with marginal credit. You're in no position to put up with overdue accounts and bad debt.

5. *Arrange to delay your payments.* Whenever you purchase anything, see if the supplier will extend terms a little longer than they initially offered. A surprising number of companies will do so to make a sale. Why don't they usually? Simple, nobody asks.

6. *Develop excellent credit.* Request that Dunn and Bradstreet develop a credit rating for your startup. Receiving an "excellent" rating will make it easier to convince other companies to provide you with longer terms. Unfortunately, establishing this rating may require initially paying some suppliers up front, but try to make the fewest number of prepayments for the least possible dollars to get the rating you need.

7. *Use credit cards in a disciplined fashion.* The beauty of credit cards is that they provide extra time to float expenses – no questions asked. You purchase something, then later get the bill, then later pay it. With that said, try to pay off the entire balance. Do not use credit cards as a loan that you must pay interest on if the numbers don't justify it.

8. *Barter.* Bartering is a great way to reduce expenses. In fact, it can be such a powerful tool that it can fundamentally help shape your initial business idea. There might be some large cost that you can avoid throughout the life of the business that fundamentally improves the economics of your business model.

But, like any other technique, there are better and worse ways to barter. First, try to barter with individuals who would not ordinarily purchase your product or service. You don't want to cannibalize real cash sales if you can avoid it. Second, try to give away something that costs you little, but might have great value to the other party.

I followed these principles in a commuter airline that I once managed. We got a tremendous amount of freebees by bartering. What did we barter? We could let people fly standby free. It cost us nothing but the travel had tremendous value to suppliers. We got discounts on fuel. We got free advertising. We received furniture at cost. You name it. It was amazing. And none of these people would have paid cash to fly with us. So my question is – what can you trade or barter that might cost you little or nothing, but has great value to your vendors or other people you do business with?

9. *Negotiate, negotiate, and then negotiate.* It is amazing what you can get if you ask. Make it a practice to get a better deal whenever you can. Always try. Saving an average of five percent on every purchase might double your first year's profits. Remember, you can negotiate four issues, each of which can help your cash flow: you can pay suppliers less or later, or you can charge customers more or collect sooner. If you have no success in one area, try another.

10. *When you have the cash, don't spend it.* One crucial piece of advice is to keep it lean even if you come into some extra money. Regardless of whether the cash comes from a few good months of sales or a wealthy investor, don't start spending freely. The huge office, new furniture, and expensive trips can all wait until you're on very firm ground. Stroking your ego with extravagant purchases can come back to haunt you.

11. *Consider hiring student interns.* You might want to utilize student interns or college class teams for certain tasks. To successfully recruit a good intern, you need to emphasize whichever of the following benefits are applicable: the possibility of hiring them, the opportunity to be mentored, the chance to gain high-level experience that will qualify them for higher level positions, flexible hours, and a chance to apply their academic skills. Many faculty will let you visit their classes to briefly present your internship opportunity. This approach is almost guaranteed to lead to getting a better student than merely posting a description somewhere.

12. *Practice controlled growth.* Remember, the difficulty of funding growth is one of the main reasons why companies run out of money. Growth can also be a huge stressor and eat up any free time you would have had. At the same time, some growth is not only necessary, it is a key to financial success. Thus, you not only want to be reasonably careful about how quickly you grow, but far more importantly, you want to sieze only the right growth opportunities. Don't, for example, pursue low margin prospects that involve activities you detest. You'll do more than damage your cash flow, you'll quite possibly wreck your life!

## Variable Costs or Fixed Costs

In addition to the actions above, there is one more major way to adjust your cost structure to make sure you will be able to pay your bills, sleep peacefully, and enjoy a life outside of your business. It relates to whether most of your expenses are variable or fixed. Almost every single book or instructional guide on entrepreneurship defines these terms, but they don't explain whether one cost structure is better than the other, and if so, how to attain that cost structure. That omission can lead to unexpectedly running out of money, miserable times and possibly even business failure.

I will define the terms variable and fixed costs in case they're new to you. A **variable cost** is a cost that changes in direct proportion to revenue. If your variable costs are 50% of revenue, one dollar in sales will generate a variable cost of $0.50. If you achieve sales of $10,000, your corresponding variable cost will be $5,000. A **fixed cost** stays the same regardless of revenue. If you make $10,000 in sales your fixed cost will be $5,000. If you make $15,000 in sales, your fixed costs would still be $5,000.

Now, let's walk through an example. You expect $1,000,000 in sales in your first year and you have a variable cost of $0.50 per dollar. What are your variable costs? If you answered $500,000, excellent – you're correct.

Now, let's assume you still expect $1,000,000 in sales but you've somehow shifted your costs so they are entirely fixed. Further, assume your fixed costs are $450,000. So you would be spending $500,000 if you use variable costs and just $450,000 if you use fixed costs, so it looks like the fixed cost option would save you $50,000.

So that means, of course, you should use fixed cost option. Right? Wrong – absolutely – positively – wrong.

Early in a venture life, you want to avoid fixed costs like the plague. Use variable costs whenever possible. Why? The scenario I just described stated, "you **expect** $1,000,000 in sales." The important word was "expect." How hard did we decide it was to accurately project first year sales? If your answer is "almost impossible", you're absolutely right.

Though I've consulted, taught, and had my own businesses, even my projections are often off. Yours will be too. Venture capitalists aren't accurate. Banks aren't accurate. And entrepreneurs especially aren't accurate. Remember the statistics at the start of the chapter, not only are entrepreneurs almost always wrong, they are wrong by a lot and they are too optimistic.

So, how does the difficulty of estimating sales relate to deciding whether to choose a variable or fixed cost structure? Simply stated, in sharp contrast to variable costs, fixed costs can cause your company to go bankrupt if you overestimate sales.

Assume that you estimate $1,000,000 in sales and you have $450,000 in fixed costs. At the end of the year, you may find out you've only sold $400,000 worth of goods. That happens all the time. The end result – you're $50,000 in the red. You work countless hours to try to recover. Your marriage is falling apart because you are so stressed out. Ultimately your business fails.

Instead, if you had utilized variable costs at .50 per dollar of sales, the outcome would've been very different. Assume again, $400,000 in sales rather than the million you expected. But this time, since variable costs are just half of actual sales, your costs are just $200,000. This means you make $200,000. Sure you may be a little disappointed, but you turned a profit. You can pay your suppliers, and your wife or husband hasn't left you.

So, whenever possible, use variable costs.

Of course, you may be thinking, but don't entrepreneurs sometimes have more sales than they anticipate? Yes – sometimes. And, if you follow the principles in this book you are far more likely to fall into that happy category.

Let's for a moment assume that instead of making $1,000,000 in sales, much to your delight you make $2,000,000. If you had picked the fixed cost option you would have only $450,000 worth of expenses. You would have earned a $1,550,000 profit.

Uh-oh, if you picked the variable cost option, you would have had $2,000,000 in sales and $1,000,000 in expenses. That means you only make $1,000,000.

Sorry, but I'm just not shedding tears because you **only** cleared a million dollars. Either way, you are a millionaire. And remember very, very few entrepreneurs underestimate sales, while over 90% overestimate sales substantially. The simple table that follows should illustrate why it is so important to utilize variable costs when possible.

## Consequences of Misjudging Sales

|  | Overestimate Sales | Underestimate Sales |
|---|---|---|
| **Variable cost business** | Result: You will have made the most money possible, although given disappointing sales it will be less than expected. You will be profitable.<br><br>Frequency of this result: Very frequent.<br><br>Adjustment: None needed. | Result: You will not have made the most money possible, but you would still earn more than you expected to originally.<br><br>Frequency of this result: Very infrequent.<br><br>Adjustment: Next year change to fixed cost structure to maximize earnings. |
| **Fixed cost business** | Result: You will not have made the most money possible and most likely will have lost money.<br><br>Frequency of this result: Very frequent.<br><br>Adjustment: Next year if possible, consider changing to variable cost structure to maximize earnings. | Result: You will have made the most money possible, far more than you expected to originally.<br><br>Frequency of this result: Very infrequent.<br><br>Adjustment: None needed. |

So bottom line, the upside of selecting variable costs is they are likely to lead you to make a profit, save you a great deal of agony and let you live a decent life. The downside is that there is a small chance you may not make as much as you might have, although it will still be more than you anticipated. In the unlikely case that this occurs, you can shift over to a fixed cost model next year.

In contrast, you could have chosen fixed costs initially. But the downside of choosing fixed costs initially is huge and is very likely to occur. The choice can lead to financial ruin.

Of course, one cannot always choose between fixed and variable costs. There are, however, a surprising number of times when that choice exists. For example, you can:

1. pay salespeople commission rather than salaries
2. subcontract manufacturing rather than buying expensive equipment to produce your product
3. rather than hiring your own employees, outsource support functions like payroll to organizations that charge based upon volume
4. form alliances with other companies where they help sell your product for a piece of the action
5. avoid major large purchases of advertising with traditional media which require that you pay a set fee. Instead, buy advertising where you pay a percentage of the sales it generates.

Closely related to the tactic of replacing fixed costs with variable costs is the tactic of avoiding inflexible long term financial obligations in favor of more flexible alternatives. For example, you can:

1. rent space initially rather than buy
2. lease equipment rather than buy
3. employ contract labor rather than hiring employees

4. raise money through equity or profit sharing rather than taking on debt with its fixed interest payments (more on this in the next chapter).

## Refining The Idea

Let's say you consider applying as much of the previous advice as you can, and still conclude that your business idea entails too large an investment or too likely a need for constant cash infusions. If that is the case, you might need to fundamentally refine your business idea. Much like in previous chapters, several options are possible.

1. *Try another idea.* You might decide to abandon your idea if it is inevitable that you will be starting a business with awful cash flow ramifications. Yes, cash flow is that important. But only choose this alternative if you have other business ideas that are very appealing to you.

2. *Narrow your business's scope.* Are there certain activities that your idea contains that have awful cash flow ramifications? Can you shed the business of those activities? In a sense, Julie did this when she avoided producing her own organic food. The time lag between growing a crop and selling the food is extensive. In contrast, by purchasing foods from farmers and delivering it, she had almost no gap between paying suppliers and getting paid by customers.

3. *Partner.* This alternative might go hand in hand with the one above. After narrowing your scope, you may choose to work closely with a business that performs the "missing" activities. The partner may be in a much better position to handle tasks with poor cash flow ramifications because they have substantial resources or have already made the needed investment.

Let me use books, or for that matter, any product that is primarily distributed and marketed via the internet, as an example. After developing the product, the producer can market it on his or her own. This process, however, requires building a website, developing a list of interested clientele, and attracting a massive amount of traffic to the site. This can take months, if not longer, and can become expensive.

The alternative is to partner with an "affiliate". Many affiliates have already invested years in developing a huge list of loyal clients with a specific interest that coincides with your book's topic. The affiliate emails everyone on their list information about your book or product and gets a percent for every client who purchases. They get paid exactly when you do. You've basically replaced the up front fixed cost of building a website and developing your own list with a variable cost. While eventually you want to develop your own lists and website, working with an affiliate might be the perfect way to start. Think about similar types of arrangements that might fit your business idea.

4. *Service another group.* Your distribution channel may have awful cash flow ramifications because of the customers you target. A U.S. importer of floor tile, named China International Trade Associates (CITA), serves as a case in point. When I began advising this startup, a factory located in the People's Republic of China (PRC) was selling them upscale ceramic floor tile, which CITA then sold to U.S. wholesalers. CITA's up front costs were huge. Before CITA's customers made a buying decision, CITA had to pay for the tile, inventory storage, and expensive advertising in trade magazines, as well as travel all around the country

to help wholesalers convince architects to use the tile in their projects.

Making matters worse, it took an incredibly long time for CITA to collect any money from customers. Architects would decide, prior to starting to construct a building, that they wanted CITA's tile, but would not place an order at that time. They would wait, often over a year later, until the buildings were close to complete and the tile was ready to be laid. The architects then ordered the tile from the wholesaler and the wholesaler then placed the order with CITA. The wholesaler would pay CITA 30 to 60 days after that. What a cash flow nightmare!

The solution? Instead of targeting architects and wholesalers as customers, CITA targeted U.S. tile manufacturers. This allowed CITA to focus more on its ability to source tile at a very low cost, based upon their unique long-term relationship with factories in the PRC. CITA arranged for the factory in the PRC to sell directly to U.S. manufacturers. For CITA's service as a middleman (which was protected by a contract), the company received 20% of the price the U.S. manufacturer paid the factory in the PRC. The U.S. manufacturers oversaw and paid all costs associated with storing and marketing the tile. CITA's investment – almost nothing.

Examining the organic food industry also can illustrate how some suppliers have improved cash flow by targeting the right group of customers. Some organic farmers focus on "hardcore" organic customers. These customers are willing to pay the farmer at the beginning of the season for a percentage of the crop. This practice provides money to farmers early in the growing cycle so they can pay for the supplies they need to grow food.

In closing, no book about ideas for new ventures would be complete if it did not discuss "how to obtain the capital you need to fund the idea." Unfortunately though, most books focus exclusively on the less important part of the phrase, namely, "how to obtain the capital." This chapter takes an opposite tactic, and emphasizes the more important part of the phrase, "capital you will need to fund the idea." Specifically, I argue that minimizing the amount you will need is key to being a balanced entrepreneur.

The above paragraph notwithstanding, how to obtain capital is, of course, worthy of discussion. The next chapter therefore, emphasizes many facts about getting capital that others don't mention. Specifically, it will:

1.  Specify two funding sources that few entrepreneurs consider, yet are the most likely to fund early stage entrepreneurs.
2.  Identify one funding source that is not only likely to provide you with money, but also quite likely to decrease your idea's risks, increase your enjoyment and generate more profits.
3.  Explain how to stop the funding sources you are most likely to use from turning into the single biggest regret of your life – literally.

● ● ●

# CHAPTER SUMMARY

## Major Ideas

This chapter emphasizes that the key to success is making sure your business can prosper even if your sales projections are off. You can do this by minimizing your up front and operating costs and when possible, replacing fixed costs with variable costs. If employing the suggested tactics don't look like they will do enough to ensure that your idea will generate a positive cash flow, the chapter discusses four ways you can refine the idea. Importantly, the chapter also stresses that decreasing your need for external financing is key to being a balanced entrepreneur.

• • •

Go to **TheBalancedEntrepreneur.com** for exercises, research and readings related to minimizing your need for financing.

Just click on the tab labeled "Resources".

CHAPTER

# FINANCING II:
## Raising Money
## More Easily

• • •

**Outdated Strategy:**
Focus on targeting banks, friends and family to fund my idea.

**New "Balanced Entrepreneur" Strategy 9:**
Focus on more creative sources.

• • •

Historically, early stage entrepreneurs approach banks, friends and family before almost any other funding sources. While we have no doubt that some entrepreneurs will have to utilize these sources, this chapter will make the case that there are better alternatives they should explore thoroughly first.

Let's assume you plan to follow the advice in the previous chapter to minimize your need for external funds, but still conclude that you will require some financing to get started. But where to get it?

The answer: NOWHERE! DON'T GET IT!

At least, not until you have done a little more thinking about each and every suggestion the previous chapter made. Yes, you plan on following some of the advice, but what more can you do?

It is truly amazing how much so many have accomplished despite starting with little or no external financing. Apple started in a garage and Dell began in a college dorm room. Ever hear of EDS? The founder, Ross Perot, invested $1,000 to launch it, yet managed to turn the company into a multibillion dollar enterprise. And if you don't have $1,000 to spare, you can emulate Paul Mitchell and John Paul DeJoria, who spent just $700 when they started Paul Mitchell Systems. It became the largest U.S. based, salon-only hair care company. Taking out no loans, they generated a combined net worth of over three billion dollars. Not a bad return on an initial investment of $700. Not only is it possible to fund ventures with just internal finances, doing so will increase how much you enjoy the entrepreneurial experience.

There are two primary sources of financing, debt and equity, and both can be dreadful. Seeking debt to finance your venture means making fixed payments to pay back the loan. As discussed, fixed costs greatly increase the riskiness of your venture. It also frequently requires providing collateral, like the very home you are living in. Not surprisingly, having your house on the line tends to increase your stress level and decrease your enjoyment.

Entrepreneurs can also trade ownership or equity for cash. Investors are quick to explain that more cash up front may generate a disproportionate amount of growth. They assert, "Owners would rather have 51% of a billion dollar business, than 100% of a ten thousand dollar business." But such statements don't consider many factors. First, many businesses can grow quickly without seeking additional investment by substituting creativity for cash. Second, by bringing in additional owners you may lose much of your autonomy, which may have been the main reason you wanted to be an entrepreneur in the first place.

Finally, before giving up ownership, you need to realize that your experience can quickly become unpleasant if you and the new co-owner(s) have different goals and values. As explained earlier, founders want money, but they also seek many other benefits from their venture. Four of these benefits, in order of importance, are to:

1. control their own activities at work,
2. increase their financial security,
3. have time for personal and family life, and
4. be challenged.

The four benefits an investor typically wants, in order of importance, are:

1. money
2. money
3. money, and
4. money.

Nothing wrong with that, but you can see where many conflicts can occur.

This conflict is especially likely to arise when investors want to convert their equity back into cash, so they can realize a return on their investment. It is rare for a business to generate enough funds from ongoing operations to provide a return that appropriately compensates an early investor for his or her risk. Instead, the most frequently used cash-out route is to sell the business to another entity. But this almost always requires the entrepreneur to give up control of his or her business, and more than likely leave the company entirely.

Despite its significant drawback, I don't want to paint a totally negative picture of obtaining financing. Either form of financing might be absolutely necessary to starting your business, or possibly to growing at the rate you would like. Debt, although potentially adding great risk, usually allows you the freedom to operate as you please, providing you do not run into problems repaying the loan. Furthermore, you have rights to all profits above and beyond your interest payments.

Equity also has its positive points. Although you have to share in profits and may lose some autonomy, equity allows you to avoid fixed interest payments. Perhaps even more importantly, investors can bring valuable experience, connections, and resources to your business. Furthermore, many entrepreneurs have a love of starting up companies, but lose interest when it comes to long-term management. Thus, eventually selling the company may represent an ideal outcome for all parties involved.

When deciding between debt and equity, consider the potential source of equity. Can they provide benefits other than cash? What are their goals and values? How and when do they envision getting a return on their investment? Choosing an equity investor can be as complicated as choosing a spouse, and almost as important!

## Specific Funding Sources

The good news is, there are hundreds of books published on how entrepreneurs can raise capital. The bad news is that most of these books may not meet your needs for three reasons:

1. The advice they give may not be appropriate for entrepreneurs who are just beginning their companies.

2. They do not emphasize the financing sources that best facilitate your getting all the benefits you want out of your venture.

3. While many cover the fundamentals of how you might get financing, they tend to ignore creative sources of financing or creative ways to minimize the negative impact of certain financing sources.

The remainder of this chapter will focus on filling the gaps caused by these three omissions, rather than on providing a comprehensive review of the many funding sources available. I will also list several sources from best to worst from the standpoint of being a "balanced entrepreneur." Admittedly, however, the quality of the source might vary somewhat based upon your unique situation. In the process, this chapter will show that being creative in your search for money often minimizes some of the drawbacks associated with getting funding.

## Best Funding Sources

**Decreasing the Need for Funding.** Okay, you've already heard this advice, and technically decreasing the amount of funding you require is not a funding source. Suffice it to say, I believe this is the first option you should choose if possible.

**Sell Assets.** Depending upon your life situation, selling assets could very well be one of your best options. Rather than being saddled with debt or having to give away part of your business, so many of us have items we can live without. Do you have any of the following: cars, pool tables, second properties, boats, excess furniture or jewelry? Are some of these items just sitting around gathering dust? How much would you miss them if they were gone?

Cars, in particular, may provide a nice option. If you have an expensive, fairly new car, think about selling it. You could lease something less extravagant. This one sacrifice might provide you with $15,000 to $20,000 up front.

Let's get even a little more dramatic. Does it make sense for you to sell your house? Is now a good time to downsize? Are there several rooms you never use? Have the kids gone off to college, so you no longer need to live in a town with the best school system? Just how much might you clear by moving to a smaller place in a less prestigious location: $100,000 – more – less? Obviously, before pursuing this option, you need to weigh and consider many factors, including trends in the local real estate market.

Asset lease backs are another option that don't trap you into a loan and let you avoid giving up ownership in your business. Do you have a business asset or assets, such as real estate or computer equipment, that you can sell to a friend or relative? They, in turn, could lease it back to your business. The friend or relative gets a stream of revenue, a tax deduction, and possible use of assets when the lease runs out. You receive a lump of cash and possibly a better leasing deal than would be available elsewhere. An important additional benefit is that in many cases the arrangement won't affect your liabilities or equity, so it would not interfere with getting financing in the future if needed. (Consult with an accountant to structure your arrangement to meet these criteria.)

**Strategic Partnerships:** Securing funds from a strategic partner is among the best options you have, and one entrepreneurs almost never pursue. A strategic partnership is an alliance between two companies, usually involving a contract. The underlying premise is that the companies contain assets or strengths that can be shared for the benefit of both companies. These partnerships may take many forms. A larger firm, for example, may supply capital and marketing assistance, while the smaller firm supplies technological or creative expertise.

You may gain a multitude of benefits from a strategic partner, including shared space, legitimacy, equipment and, of course, capital. A strategic partner might be willing to provide you with cash at a lower interest rate or for less equity than others, because they have a vested interest in your success. By sharing some resources, you may be able to minimize the amount of cash you need as well. The partnership could be with a potential supplier, prospective customer, complementary company, or any one of a number of other possibilities.

Learning Production illustrates how one startup successfully formed a partnership with a future customer. The company's two founders, Scott Mitchell and Steve Goodman, were developing a training software application that simulates actual business experiences. Although they had no finished products, they went on an exploratory sales call to a potential customer. By the end of the meeting, without even being asked, the customer indicated it was interested in far more than just making a purchase when the software was done. After negotiating a mutually beneficial agreement, it supplied startup capital, office space and access to computer equipment. Mitchell explained, "By having our initial financing come from our first client, we knew our product was going to be useful."

Future suppliers might also be viable sources of capital. To sweeten the pot, you could promise to purchase their products. You can get more creative and ask whether, in exchange for equity, you can lease a supplier's equipment at very favorable rates, or even get free goods. In fact, a whole sub-industry, venture leasing, has arisen around this very idea, although admittedly at this point the leasing firms are primarily only interested in very large scale startups, with very experienced top management teams. The main message is, once again, be creative.

Suppliers who meet any of the criteria below may be especially likely to work with you.

1. Your future purchases might account for a large portion of their revenue.
2. They have low variable costs and high fixed costs. This cost structure makes securing future customers especially important.
3. They have excess cash they could invest.
4. They have excess inventory which they can trade for equity.

In addition to potential suppliers and customers, companies who have products that complement yours might make great partners. Complementary products are goods that get consumed together. Sales of your product might help them sell more of theirs. Just a few of the multitude of pairs of complementary products include hotdogs and buns, software and computers, and personal financial planning and legal services.

You can be quite creative in developing your list of companies. Someone starting a business selling high end sporting goods might, for example, attract customers who are also interested in personal fitness training, sports therapy, and nutritional advice. You can offer businesses supplying these services referrals, in addition to, or instead of, equity or interest payments, if they provide some startup cash.

Although strategic partnerships, especially when they involve equity, might cost you some autonomy, they have many advantages. Securing funding through a strategic partnership may lead to synergies far into the future, allowing for a stress free enjoyable business for years to come.

## Good Funding Sources

**Microloans.** Microloans are another very promising but under-utilized source of funds for startups. Microloans are very small loans to small business borrowers that are usually given at the startup stage for the purpose of spurring entrepreneurship. A wide range of organizations including informal financial service providers, formal financial service institutions, member owned organizations, and non-governmental organizations all provide microloans. The Small Business Administration started a micro-lending program in 1992, which it made permanent in 1997. It uses nonprofit intermediaries to make loans to new and existing borrowers.

One specific type of microloan involves "peer to peer" lending. Rather than going through a bank, one can post a loan request on a website, where many private investors can view it. Some of these sites facilitate auctions, whereby the lender who charges the lowest interest rate will win your loan. Often you do not need to provide security or collateral, and can very much be in the startup stage of the business. Two companies that facilitate peer to peer lending are The Lending Club (www.lendingclub.com/home.action) and Prosper (www.prosper.com).

Most microloan programs furnish capital to companies that can't get access to funds from other more traditional sources, for one of three reasons. They are startups, too small, and/or may have founders who have had minor past credit problems. Two additional advantages that micro lenders have over traditional lenders, is that they often offer more flexible loan terms and may accept a wider range of assets as collateral. It is not unheard of for a microlender to sanction the use of office equipment, or even the owner's home washer and dryer, to secure a loan.

You should be aware, though, that these loans have downsides, including charging a higher interest rate than standard business loans. Furthermore, depending upon which micro lender you approach, it may take as long as a bank to make a loan decision. Also, the amount one can borrow is often low, usually ranging from as little as $100 to a maximum of $50,000.

It may also be difficult to find the ideal micro lender. Often they only distribute funds in their own communities and/or regions (especially when they are sponsored by the SBA). You may need the assistance of a business support group with ties to micro lenders to locate the lenders. AmeriCorps, for example, dispenses small loans to companies that work in disaster areas. Two micro lenders are Accion Texas (http://www.acciontexas.org/) and Self-Help (http://www.self-help.org/).

## Risky Funding Sources That You May Have To Use

**Bank Loans.** Frequently, founders go to a bank for a loan to start their company. This often turns into a very frustrating experience because banks usually try to avoid funding startups and are much more likely to deal with established companies. Furthermore, in the unlikely event that the bank officer considers making a loan to a startup, he or she will probably demand that the entrepreneur meet at least two of the three following conditions:

1. That the entrepreneur personally guarantees the loan. This means he or she is responsible for paying even if the business cannot.

2. That the entrepreneur provides collateral. Collateral often is property, such as a home, that serves as security for the loan. If the founder fails to pay the loan, the bank gets to keep the collateral.

3. The bank may request that the entrepreneur provide a loan guarantee from a third party. A loan guarantee occurs when a third party agrees to repay all or part of a loan in the event that the borrower defaults. The Small Business Administration (SBA) might be a source of a third party loan guarantee. It can warrant up to 80% of a loan value, but is very selective in choosing the startups they support. They might guarantee loans between $35,000 and $350,000.

The combination of shelling out fixed interest payments, providing personal guarantees, and possibly losing your collateral make bank loans very risky. In contrast to equity investors, however, lenders are much more likely to provide you the freedom to manage your business as you see fit.

You can save a lot of time by prequalifying banks. Specifically, when approaching a bank, right after identifying yourself, ask about the criteria below:

1. The size of the loan they might grant. Smaller institutions tend to have capital constraints that restrict the size of loans they make. Larger institutions sometimes have a per transaction minimum.

2. The industries in which the bank typically gives loans. It is more difficult to get a bank to grant a loan in industries that are unfamiliar to them.

3. The geographic locations in which the bank prefers to grant loans. Banks within the federal system receive Community

Reinvestment Act credits for lending within their geographical charter area and debits for lending outside it. The challenge of dealing with varied collection laws and other local regulations makes many regional banks unwilling to lend outside certain areas.

Websites, such as iBank.com and TheStreet.com (TSCM), can help you compare and prequalify banks.

**Friends and Family.** Other than from the founders themselves, the most frequent source of seed capital or startup funding is from friends or family. This funding may come in the form of debt or equity.

There are many advantages to obtaining funds from friends and family, not the least of which is that they may come through for you with money in many situations where others will not. They know you and may have faith in your abilities. When other sources may be rejecting your proposal left and right because you or the business lack a 'relevant' track record and/or you have no collateral, friends or family members may believe that you can be successful.

They may also want to support you for emotional reasons; they are legitimately interested in your well being. You may be able to quickly and easily forge an agreement as they don't necessarily need to run credit checks and may not ask you for collateral.

Before you celebrate though, there are also significant disadvantages when seeking funds from friends and family. For example, you might feel very uncomfortable requesting funds. Also, depending upon who they are, their finances may limit the amount you can raise; and, if you need more funds later, their pockets may be empty. In addition, they may not be able to provide you with expert business advice or an extensive network of contacts, like some other potential investors can.

But by far, the biggest drawback, and the main reason why I consider friends and family a "risky funding source", is that you are jeopardizing a close personal relationship. A big part of enjoying your life outside of your business is enjoying great times with friends and family, and to do that you need to keep your friends and be on speaking terms with your family. Despite what you think at the start, you could very easily lose a best friend, or never be able to look your sister and brother-in-law in the eye again. No matter how bad you might feel about being unable to repay a bank loan, it won't compare to the misery associated with losing the money of someone you love. And they might not be too happy with the situation either.

*Structuring the agreement.* The good news is that you can structure your agreement so that it radically increases the odds of maintaining a positive relationship. The first step is deciding who to ask for the money. Or perhaps more accurately stated, who not to ask. Be selective about who you approach. If you want a good life, don't solicit people who can ill afford to give. Sure, in general you could let the buyer (or financier) beware, but these are people to whom you're close.

Plus, you're not just protecting them, you're also making sure that things stay pleasant for you. If a person who can't afford it provides funds, there's no end to the ugliness that might arise. Do you really want calls months before a payment is due asking you if you can find it in your heart to pay in advance? After all, he was there for you when you needed it and is now about to be evicted from his apartment. And heaven forbid, suppose you are a little late with a payment one time.

Let's be honest though. Some people can afford to make a loan, but will still be pains. You know who they are. Don't go to them for money. Life is short! I know you want the money, but pay attention to your instincts.

Because approaching loved ones puts so much at risk, my advice is to go to them as a last resort, when it doesn't look like you can get all the funds you need in any other way. And sorry, but since you are out of options, they are doing you the favor, not the reverse. That means that they need a reasonable return on their money. If, for example, a bank just turned you down for a loan at 8%, and you are out of options, should you really give a friend less than 8%?

Even if you have to approach friends and family for money, if at all possible, try to get at least some of your funding from unbiased outside sources first. This lets you benchmark a fair return. Furthermore, it shows your loved ones that you are approaching them with a worthwhile investment, rather than making them feel like they are doing you a favor (Yes, I know I'm contradicting the paragraph above, just don't let them know that.)

If at all possible, I strongly recommend that you try to structure the deal as a loan rather than equity. A relationship combining business with friendship and/or love is already difficult enough, so at least try to keep the business part simple. And debt is much simpler than equity. Do you really want your mom giving you "advice" about maximizing the business's returns, or your brother-in-law "inquiring" about how he can get his money out of the deal?

In fact, you might even want to go one step beyond requesting a loan rather than offering equity. Consider asking your friend or family to provide a loan guarantee instead of a loan. You gain several advantages, not the least of which is, many individuals might be better able to provide the guarantee. Even if the person has a high net worth, his or her money may be tied up. Since someone providing a loan guarantee only needs to expend cash if you run into problems, the guarantor may not need to be quite as liquid. Perhaps, though, the main benefit of the arrangement is that it minimizes the amount you have to interact with the cosigner about your business. Assuming you repay the bank loan on time, your cosigner never needs to get involved.

Regardless of how you structure the agreement, build in a safety margin if you can. If you think you can begin to repay a loan in three months after starting your company, try to negotiate starting your payments in six months. Also, specify quarterly rather than monthly payments, so you are less subject to monthly fluctuation. After figuring out the maximum amount you can pay per quarter, try agreeing to a much lower dollar figure over a longer payback time. Once the business starts, one of your highest priorities should be to set aside what is owed and make larger payments sooner than promised. Surpass minimum requirements. That is how you can hold your head high at family reunions or when drinking with friends at the bar.

*Do you need it in writing?* Your parents have been with you since the day you were born. Perhaps your friend was your maid of honor and the person with whom you share all your most private thoughts. Or maybe your buddy is an old army pal who saved your life. Obviously, you do not need a written agreement with these individuals as much as you need it with strangers. Right?

Wrong, 100% wrong. While you **always** need a written agreement, the closer the relationship, the more important it is. Why? Having a written document might do more than save a good business relationship, it might save the far more important personal relationship. A balanced entrepreneur doesn't let business hurt friendships or weaken family ties.

It is not a matter of trust. It is a matter of understanding. Can a person really be aware of all the nuances of an agreement if it is not written down? Two years down the road, will she accurately remember everything which was discussed and be able to distinguish items tentatively proposed from items which were firmly agreed upon? Will you?

Make the document a formal one, and make sure all parties grasp the details. Run it by a lawyer and accountant. Loans necessitate a promissory note, agreed to by the borrower. Among other things, detail the interest rate, the repayment plan, the type of security if any, and the ramifications of early payments. If you have no choice but to offer equity, you need to write a stock purchase agreement which spells out all the details. Even if a person wants to give you funds as a gift, you still want him or her to write a letter explaining this. When you formalize the agreement, both parties feel more confident because expectations are clear and everybody's interests are protected.

Additionally, having a clear cut agreement will save you hassles if you seek future funds from lenders and investors. They won't give you a penny unless you can show them exactly what you owe, and to whom. Inconsistencies, vagueness, or sloppiness about the terms of previous deals will delay or even cost you current possibilities. Talk about adding major, needless future obstacles to your business's success and personal happiness.

Have the loan managed by an intermediary to keep the relationship on a professional level. These companies handle many aspects of the relationship, even including details like sending an email to remind you that an electronic funds transfer to your lender's bank is about to occur. One of several companies that administers loans between friends and/or families members is Zimple Money (http://www.zimplemoney.com/Family-Friend-Loan.aspx).

*Making the request.* Let's face it. Asking friends and/or relatives for money can be awkward. Here are some tactics which might make the task a bit less onerous.

1. Use email to start the process. Email allows you to reach many people and initially keeps it informal. Mention the idea and the benefit to potential funders in very general terms.

2. Before soliciting a meeting, first ask if parties are interested in receiving a business plan or some other relevant material. Then follow up with those who wanted the materials.

3. Some "authorities" suggest asking for general advice about your business rather than initially making it clear that you are soliciting funds. This approach might be fine if approaching a person with a specialized knowledge base from whom you truly want advice. I don't, however, recommend the technique if you are solely using it as a ploy to raise funds. It can become awkward and sets the wrong tone if the person does end up supplying funds. You are sending a signal that they have more of a say in running the business than you will actually grant them.

4. While I don't necessarily recommend asking for general business advice, do request advice related to raising the funds. In addition to asking if the party you are emailing might be interested, request the names of any contacts they have who might want to investigate the opportunity.

5. Offer the potential backer a range of amounts they might provide. This avoids the awkward situation in which you have misjudged their lending capacity.

Regardless of how you go about seeking capital, it's important to remember that you are approaching friends and family because often other sources won't provide you with startup capital based on your own merit. You need to really think about the risks inherent in your business idea before asking someone you love to give you money. To put it bluntly, I personally would only approach them if I were closely adhering to the principles in this book that reduce risk.

## More about Sources of Financing

This chapter has focused on five sources of financing that are most available for companies in the startup phase. Arguably, entrepreneurs all too often overlook three of these, namely strategic partnerships, microloans, and selling personal assets. The chapter also discusses how entrepreneurs can keep life pleasant as they solicit and secure funds from friends and family.

There are many other financing sources that I am not going to discuss in depth, because they usually only serve established firms, generate huge risks, or only support a very small percent of all who approach them. These sources are worth a brief mention though.

1. Insurance policies: You can often borrow against a whole-life insurance policy, if you have had the policy for three or more years. You just need to write a note to your agent or insurance company, requesting a policy loan. Most companies will grant you up to 90 percent of the cash value of the policy, charging an interest rate which is reasonable. The main drawbacks parallel those of any loan, but in addition, your death benefits might be diminished if you die with the loan outstanding. Of course, the biggest problem is that most founders do not have an established whole life policy to borrow against.

2. Your 401(k). Although it depends upon the plan, you may be able to borrow against the 401(k) retirement plan you have with your current or former employer. There are, however, often many constraints attached to these loans. You may:

   a. be subject to large penalty fees if you don't repay the loan according to schedule

   b. need to keep working at your current job (so you could only pursue the venture part-time)

   c. only be allowed to borrow a small percentage of the money saved in your 401(k) – usually no more than half of your vested balance

   d. have to repay the loan incredibly quickly, sometimes within 30 days, if you lose your job.

   There is also the little detail that should your venture fail, you are putting your retirement at risk.

3. *Credit Cards.* Many entrepreneurs finance their venture with credit cards. This can be a dangerous route to go, however. Interest rates are usually quite high, and you can easily rack up a large debt and destroy your credit rating. Despite their dangers, credit cards offer the advantage of ease, accessibility and speed. You do not need to carefully prepare a massive amount of materials to apply for cards, a high percentage of individuals qualify (my niece was preapproved when she was just seven years old) and you can get approved in days.

4. *Grants.* Some startup businesses might qualify to receive grants, which are primarily provided by foundations and government agencies. By their nature, grants can only be used

to fund ventures if they operate in the area of the grant, such as improving communities, solving social issues, promoting conservation and catalyzing economic development. Grants are also often aimed at promoting technology and aiding minority entrepreneurs. You might start your search for grants at your local or state Chamber of Commerce.

5. *Angels.* Angels are affluent individuals who provide capital to new companies in exchange for ownership equity. Typical angels invest hundreds of thousands of dollars in early stage companies. Investments in pre-revenue startups are much rarer. As angel investors are often successful entrepreneurs, they can also provide valuable business advice. Over the years, angels have increasingly formed groups which assess business plans and co-invest. One of the larger organizations comprised of angels is Angel Capital Association (www.angelcapitalassociation.org).

In addition to working through angel groups, seeking out individual angels may be useful. Make use of your personal network – especially your professional advisors, such as CPAs and advisors.

6. *Venture capitalists.* Venture capitalists invest outside equity from professionally managed pools of money in exchange for part ownership. These firms are especially interested in investing millions in ventures which have the potential for explosive growth and profitability. It is unlikely that they will invest in brand new startups.

Before finishing this chapter, I feel compelled to remind you of something I said earlier. To enjoy your work and have a life outside of work, spend extensive time thinking about how you can perfect your business idea so that it minimizes the external capital you require. The next chapter summarizes this book and explains your next steps to turn your idea into your company.

• • •

## CHAPTER SUMMARY

### Major Ideas

This chapter discusses sources of funding that might be available to ventures in the startup stages. Specifically, it suggests that selling superfluous personal assets and forming strategic partnerships might be two of the most desirable options. Selling assets allows you to maintain your autonomy by keeping ownership in your hands, and it avoids the hazards associated with making fixed payments. The synergies that strategic partnerships generate might make it easier to convince a potential partner to provide funding, and also might give you a significant advantage after starting the company.

The chapter also discusses microloans, a source of funding that is relatively accessible to entrepreneurs but that they frequently overlook. After discussing the risks inherent in bank loans, I explain the friends and family alternative. While this source of funding is frequently available, it is not without its dangers; namely, getting money from a person you love can strain or even destroy the relationship. I, therefore, spend a great deal of time discussing ways to structure your financial arrangement so that it does not hurt your personal relationship. Most of the advice falls into one of two categories: keep the arrangement extremely formal, and try to make the terms as undemanding as possible, so that you can more than meet them.

• • •

Go to **TheBalancedEntrepreneur.com**
for exercises, research and readings related
to raising money more easily.

Just click on the tab labeled "Resources".

CHAPTER

# STARTING:
## Turning My Idea Into
## My Company

• • •

**Outdated Strategy:**
Do a complete thorough business plan and then run your business based on that plan.

**New "Balanced Entrepreneur" Strategy 10:**
Seamlessly merge starting your business with the planning process. The planning process should never end.

• • •

Most entrepreneurship books stress doing careful up front planning and then starting your business based on your plan. My approach is quite different: merge the planning process with the process of starting the business. Don't wait to have all the details of the plan figured out and carefully written down before you start. As I have stressed throughout this book, the most meaningful data comes not from surveys or archives but from actually trying to sell goods, so why on earth should you try to develop a complete detailed plan without the best, most meaningful information, and then stop the planning process as soon as the good data becomes available? Yet, that is what ninety-nine out of one hundred sources tell you to do. Instead, I recommend the steps below, some of which you may have already completed.

1. Generate a multitude of ideas from chapter two.
2. Collect information to refine the ideas using chapters three through eight. Remember, this includes trying to make at least some sales as early as possible, essentially starting the company before you have everything figured out.
3. As you generate sales and "real" information, reread the chapters and fine tune your answers. Which assumptions were correct and which were faulty? Try different tactics, always asking yourself whether they are generating more money and enjoyment, while requiring less time.

Obviously writing up a detailed plan may be necessary to raise funds. There are many good books out there that tell you how to do that. But remember, that plan is for the funders. What you need is to institute a continuing cycle of learning, acting, and gathering feedback.

## Legal Considerations

Early in the process of establishing this cycle, you will need to complete several steps to protect yourself legally. Legal nightmares are not a path to a better business or a better life. While rules are often specific to each state, I can still give you a general outline of what you need to do and consider. With this said, you must check on state and federal requirements prior to establishing your business.

A good site to start your search is http://www.smallbusinessnotes.com/stategovernment.html

You should also consider working with a business attorney. A good way to find a lawyer is to ask for recommendations from your accountant or business acquaintances. If in doubt about an issue, ask your lawyer. Your investment in legal fees now can help you avoid major problems later. Below I review specific legal steps you may need to take.

**Acquire your Business's Name:** You need to register your business's name with the county clerk's office. Often, the secretary of state's office can help with the name selection process. For example, it often has electronic data bases of existing names that you can use to avoid duplication or even to generate ideas. Once you've selected an available name, you need to submit fees and complete forms. The business owner can then apply at the local, county or city office for a business license.

**Business Licenses:** Your business will need a business license for tax purposes and to obtain the legal privilege of operating a business. In most states, there are several different types of business licenses, and your choice of license depends on the type of business. For example, there are different forms for starting a toy store, an accounting firm, and a real estate company. A restaurant may need health department or liquor licensing, hair stylists may need to be licensed within their profession, or a child care service may need to have special permits from social service or educational agencies. Businesses which are heavily regulated often require federal licensing. Some of the licensed industries include broadcasting, pharmaceuticals, meat preparation, and firearms.

Depending on your state and the type of business venture, you may also need a local or county license. Some of these licenses or "permissions" include:

1. a zoning compliance permit which ensures that the space you are using is properly zoned for the type of business you are conducting
2. a special authorization for operating your business out of your house
3. approval that you're meeting building codes if you are planning to alter your space to better accommodate your business's needs.

The business must also meet all environmental restrictions, including limits on emissions and traffic. Health department officials, fire department personnel, building inspectors, and pollution control employees may also need to inspect the grounds, depending on the type of business venture. Once these inspections are complete, the necessary permits can then be issued to the business.

So where to get started? A great place to begin your hunt is at your local city hall or courthouse. The city clerk should be able to direct you, and can help you with all the necessary paperwork.

**Business Registration:** Employment Identification Numbers (EINs) are used to uniquely identify a business. An EIN, or federal tax ID, as it is sometimes called, is basically a social security number for a business. It allows a business to be identified on important government forms and official documents. Oftentimes, wholesale distributors require retailers to provide their EIN before they can sell to them. The identification of the business will also ensure that the IRS has the proper information to withhold applicable taxes on earnings. The IRS website (www.irs.gov/businesses) is an excellent resource to help guide business owners through the necessary tax forms.

You need an EIN if you meet any of the conditions below:

- Your business has employees.
- Your business is a corporation or a partnership.

- You file any of these tax returns: Employment, Excise or Alcohol, Tobacco and Firearms.
- You withhold taxes on income, other than wages, paid to a nonresident alien.
- You have a Keogh plan.
- You are involved with: trusts, IRAs, exempt organization business income tax returns, estates, real estate mortgage investment conduits, nonprofit organizations, farmers' cooperatives or plan administrators.
- You provide health insurance for your employees. The EIN serves as the basis for the National Standard Employer Identifier (NSEI) which is needed for electronic health transactions.

Using phone, fax, or mail, you can easily apply for an EIN from the Internal Revenue Service. You may also submit an application on the web at https://sa2.www4.irs.gov/modiein/individual/legal-structure.jsp. Immediately upon your completion of the application, the IRS will assign your EIN. You can then save the EIN confirmation notice.

**Choosing a Legal Structure:** When forming your business, you may choose among six main legal structures. These are a sole proprietorship, a partnership, a C corporation, an S corporation, a limited liability company (LLC), and a nonprofit corporation. Information about these legal structures can be found online at government websites such as www.SBA.gov and www.irs.gov. Below I provide a short description of each type:

*Sole Proprietorship* – A business owned and managed by one person. The person is personally liable for all business debts and obligations.

*Partnership* – Two or more people share ownership of one business. Each Partner can be held responsible for the actions of the other. Since decisions are governed by a partnership agreement developed by the owners, this legal form can provide a great deal of flexibility. This agreement indicates how decisions are made, how conflicts are resolved, and other important provisions about day to day operations of the company.

*C Corporation* – A legal entity owned by shareholders. This form increases credibility with creditors, suppliers, and customers, all while limiting your liability. That is to say, owners are not automatically personally responsible for the debts and obligations of the corporation. This in turn makes it easier to raise capital. You are, however, subject to double taxation of income – the government taxes corporate earnings once, and then will tax monies passed on to you in the form of dividends from the corporation. Forming a corporation requires additional paperwork with the secretary of state's office, and can take about six weeks for approval.

*S Corporation* – S corporations are a special corporate form particularly suitable for companies with relatively few shareholders. It avoids double taxation and also allows for limited liability.

*Limited Liability Company (LLC)* – A new legal structure that provides the limited liability features of a corporation, avoids double taxation, and offers the operational flexibility of a partnership. One can choose to have it taxed as a partnership or as an S corporation.

*Non-Profit* – An organization not motivated by making a profit. Non-profits are often exempt from paying federal taxes.

Although the legal structure you choose can always be changed, you still need to try to select the best alternative to avoid later complications and expenses. All business legal structures have their own pros and cons and you are best off consulting an attorney. With that said, the tables and exercise below, adapted from the Ewing Marion Kauffman Foundation, can help guide your choice. It attempts to make sure that your business's legal structure minimizes your concerns and meshes with your business's strategy and goals.

In Step 1, answer the questions as honestly as you can, given what you know about yourself and your business right now. These answers will help you think about what is important to you in evaluating your legal structure. There are no right or wrong answers. Then use your answers in Step 1 to help you complete Step 2.

**Step 1:** Answer the questions on the chart below by circling: Yes, Maybe, or No.

## Know Yourself

| | | | |
|---|---|---|---|
| a. Do you want to have full control and a lot of autonomy over your business's direction and decision-making? | Yes | Maybe | No |
| b. Are you willing to give up some control and autonomy for the potential of higher rewards? | Yes | Maybe | No |
| c. Do you care about how the profits are disbursed—whether they flow directly to you, whether they go to shareholders, or whether they are retained in the business? Keep in mind that this decision has tax implications. | Yes | Maybe | No |
| d. Are you willing to be personally liable for debts or injuries caused by doing business? | Yes | Maybe | No |
| e. Will you need to raise money from outside sources to get your business started or help it grow? | Yes | Maybe | No |
| f. Do you have time to fulfill extra reporting requirements needed for some types of business structures? | Yes | Maybe | No |
| g. Will you need to have flexibility to change the business structure as your business changes and grows? | Yes | Maybe | No |
| h. Do you care if the business survives after your death or the death of one of the other owners? | Yes | Maybe | No |
| i. Will your profit margins be so thin or your need for profit so high that tax considerations will drive the type of business structure you choose? | Yes | Maybe | No |
| j. Might your business qualify to be a nonprofit organization? | Yes | Maybe | No |

**Step 2:** Circle the answers within the Legal Structures Comparison Table overleaf that most reflect your concerns based on the questions in Step 1 above.

**Step 3:** Review the circles on the table to determine which structure seems the best for your business. Always talk to a trusted legal adviser to review any final decisions.

**Legal protection of intellectual property.** Another important consideration is how to protect your offering through methods like patents, trademarks, service marks or copyrights. Each of these is described below.

A patent represents an exclusive right given you by the federal government for your invention for a set time period. The invention can include a new and useful process, machine, article of manufacture, or composition of matter, or any new and useful improvement thereof. This right prevents others from making, using or distributing the invention without permission. You, in turn, must publicly disclose the nature of your invention. To qualify, the invention must be new, inventive, and useful or industrially applicable. Although it varies, patents often protect inventions for upwards of 20 years and can often be registered to provide further protection.

A trademark is typically a distinctive name, word, phrase, logo, symbol, design, image, or a combination of these, to identify and distinguish products or services to consumers. Trademarks that relate to services, rather than products, are often referred to as service marks. The U.S. Patent and Trademark Office provides information on registering trademarks and patents, and can be visited at www.uspto.gov. This website contains a database of registered trademarks and offers electronic filing of trademark applications and other trademark documents.

## Legal Structures

| | Do I control the business? | What happens to the profits? | Am I responsible for financial obligations? | Is money relatively easy to raise? | Is it easy and inexpensive to get started and fulfill the legal requirements? | Can I easily change the legal structure of the business? | What happens if one of the owners dies? | What tax advantages and/or disadvantages exist? |
|---|---|---|---|---|---|---|---|---|
| **Sole Proprietor** | Yes. | Profits are all yours. | Yes. You have unlimited personal liability for business. | No. | Yes. Using this structure is relatively easy. | Yes. Requires closing existing form and starting another. | Your business dies when you die. | Taxes are easy. Allows fewer expense deductions. |
| **Partnership** | Only if your share of the partnership is greater than 50%. | Profits are split between you and partner(s) per partnership agreement. | Yes. You and your partner(s) have unlimited personal liability. | No. | Yes. Using this structure is relatively easy, but requires partnership agreement. | Yes. But it requires closing the existing form and starting another. | Partnerships die, unless otherwise specified in the partnership agreement. | Taxes are fairly easy. Allows fewer expense deductions. |
| **Corporation** | Only if you control more than 50% of the shares of stock. | Profits belong to the corporation and may be paid to shareholders as dividends. | Not directly. Liability is generally limited to the assets of the business. | Yes. Money is easier to raise. | More difficult. Requires time and money to start and to fulfill legal obligations. | No. It is difficult to change from a corporate to non-corporate structure. | Corporations survive the death of an owner. | Double taxation is disadvantage. Allows more expense deductions. |

| | Do I control the business? | What happens to the profits? | Am I responsible for financial obligations? | Is money relatively easy to raise? | Is it easy and inexpensive to get started and fulfill the legal requirements? | Can I easily change the legal structure of the business? | What happens if one of the owners dies? | What tax advantages and/or disadvantages exist? |
|---|---|---|---|---|---|---|---|---|
| S Corporation | Only if you control more than 50% of the shares of stock. | Profits go directly to the owners, split as a percentage of shares owned. | Not directly. Liability is generally limited to the assets of the business. | Yes. Money is easier to raise. | More difficult. Requires time and money to start and to fulfill legal obligations. | No. It is difficult to change from a corporate to non-corporate structure. | Corporations survive the death of an owner. | No double taxation. Allows more expense deductions. |
| Limited Liability Company (LLC) | Only if your share of the LLC is greater than 50%. | Profits are split as detailed in your operating agreement. | Your liability is limited to the assets you invested in the business. | Somewhat. Money can be raised from members. | Varies, depends upon complexity of operating agreement. | No. It is very difficult to change from an LLC to another structure. | LLCs can survive if specified by agreement or vote. | No double taxation. Allows fewer expense deductions. |
| Nonprofit Corporation | Only if you control a majority of votes on the board of directors. | Profits must be retained. So in some sense, there are no profits. | Not directly. Liability is generally limited to the assets of the business. | If approved, nonprofits can receive tax-deductible donations. | More difficult. Requires time and money and IRS approval. | No. It is difficult to change from a nonprofit to a profit structure. | Non-profits have no owners but can survive death of founder or principal. | No taxes, but still must file informational returns. |

Copyright law protects original literary, artistic and other creative works, so that its producer has power over its publication, distribution and adaptation. A copyright usually lasts for the duration of the author's lifespan plus 50 to 70 years, after which time the work is said to enter the public domain. Copyrighting work "produced" by a corporate entity, rather than by an individual, is more complex. You can register copies of work with the federal copyright office (www. copyright.gov) to protect your rights to your work.

**Additional legal requirements.** In addition to forms associated with protecting your intellectual property, there are several other requirements for launching your business. Please note the items listed below just represent a partial list of some of the more important issues. You need to consult an accountant and/or attorney, but this represents a good starting point.

The Internal Revenue Service (IRS) requires you to fill out forms for employees. Just a few of these include:

- An I-9, which validates that the employee can legally work in the U.S.
- A W-4, which indicates the amount of income to withhold from the employee for income tax.
- A W-2, which reports annual income taxes paid and withheld.
- Forms 940 and 941, to allocate unemployment benefits if the employee loses his or her job.

You must also make sure your business has proper insurance. One form is workers' compensation insurance. This protection helps to pay injured employees' lost wages and other benefits covered by state law. Your business may also need general liability insurance, which protects against injuries on the business premises and against claims made relating to defective products or services purchased from the business.

## An Ounce of Prevention

When it comes to following the law and government regulations, an individual striving to be a balanced entrepreneur is **not** better off asking for forgiveness than permission! Why? Simple, the government doesn't forgive. Not to mix my metaphors, but you need to realize that an ounce of prevention is worth a pound of cure. Take the time now to talk to the right accountants, lawyers and insurance people before you run into trouble. Being a balanced entrepreneur means making the right trade-offs. Don't try to save yourself a little time and expense at the start on issues like the ones above, because doing so can turn your life into a nightmare later. Failure to start properly can lead to heavy fines, large lawsuits, and being shut down.

## Book Summary

Completing the nuts and bolts tasks outlined above, combined with implementing the other ideas in this book, can lead you to the lucrative and stress free life you want. Interestingly, hundreds of books strive to teach you how to plan a venture that will be financially successful, but none teach you how to plan a venture so that it will be financially successful, enjoyable, and allow you free time outside of the business. Yet the latter two issues are as important as the first.

This book simultaneously focuses on all three issues. While I won't review the whole book here, I will briefly reinforce some of the strategies that let you simultaneously achieve multiple objectives. Early on, I suggest avoiding head to head competition with established firms, and instead suggest competing differently. Doing so allows you to be imperfect and still make money. Not needing to be perfect will decrease your stress in and out of the office. Guaranteed!

Chapter six's suggestions of focusing on a market segment and charging the full price your product or service merits leads to less work, while earning more and being pulled in fewer directions. Perhaps no other single suggestion is as likely to guarantee that you love being an entrepreneur as the suggestion to make sure you enjoy the main daily activities required by your venture. And if you think enjoying your workday isn't crucial to generating the energy and persistence you will need to maximize your income, you're wrong!

While this book tells you ways to finance your idea, it probably tells you something along a related line that is far more important: how to decrease your financial needs and the probability of running out of money. This frees up your time to run your business and make it successful rather than spending enormous amounts of energy and getting stressed out in your search for funding.

As you read this book, hopefully you've taken copious notes. But maybe you have in the back of your mind, "I'm still not 100% certain about my current business idea."

Don't get discouraged. You can make these strategies work for you in your business venture by shaping and tweaking them. Be creative. Get a mentor. Talk to others. Involve third parties who are not actively involved with you or your idea, but can help you brainstorm and can see things outside the box. Absolutely don't throw your ideas away.

I suggest that you reread this book, review your notes, and most importantly, start applying the concepts. But before you do, make sure you're ready to make more money, with less risk, while having a great time!

• • •

# CHAPTER SUMMARY

## Major Ideas

This chapter focuses on the legal steps that you may need to take to turn your idea into a reality. To summarize, you will need to:

1. Acquire your business's name
2. Obtain the relevant business licenses
3. Register your business
4. Choose a legal structure
5. Protect your intellectual property:
   a. Secure a patent
   b. Obtain a trademark or service mark for relevant company names, phrases, logos etc.
   c. Copyright original or creative works
6. Fill out employee forms
7. Obtain insurance

This chapter provides the final necessary information to turn your venture idea into freedom, fun and fortune. So get started now.

• • •

Go to **TheBalancedEntrepreneur.com**
for exercises, research and readings related
to turning your idea into your company.

Just click on the tab labeled "Resources".

# BIBLIOGRAPHY

• • •

Birley, Sue, & Westhead, Paul. (1994). *A taxonomy of business startup reasons and their impact on firm growth and size.* Journal of Business Venturing, 9(1), 7

http://www.irs.gov/businesses/index.html?navmenu=menu1

http://www.uspto.gov/main/trademarks.htm

http://money.cnn.com/magazines/fortune/fortune500/2009/ performers/industries/ profits/index.html

Internal Revenue Service. (n.d.). *Tax Information for Businesses.* http://www.irs.gov/businesses/

*My Own Business.* http://www.myownbusiness.org

SCORE. Counselors to America's Small Business. www.score.org/bp_12.html

Small Business Administration. (n.d.). www.sba.gov.

United States Copyright Office (n.d.). www.copyright.gov.

United States Patent and Trademark Office(n.d.). www.uspto.gov.

Made in United States
Orlando, FL
11 December 2022